THE TV THEME SONG
SING~ALONG SONG BOOK

By
John Javna

Designed by
Ron Addad & Roland Addad

Published by
St. Martin's Press
175 Fifth Avenue
New York, NY 10010

DEDICATED TO GORDON, who claims he reads this part. It's really his book too.

OTHER BOOKS BY JOHN JAVNA:
- *60s!* (with Gordon Javna)
- *How To Jitterbug*

THIS BOOK WAS CREATED AND PACKAGED BY J-BIRD PRESS

TYPESETTING BY: KAZAN Typeset Services
PASTE-UP BY: Vicki Rombs
MUSIC TYPESETTING BY: Ed Schilling

Sing along with us on P. 52

DESIGN BY: Ron Addad and Roland Addad (thanks, guys).
ISBN: 0-312-78215-2
Library of Congress Catalogue Number: 84-758771

15 14 13 12

A NOTE:

This volume is a TV nostalgia book. It's a little different than most, because it's got songs in it. But the purpose is the same as other nostalgia books — to preserve memories of America's favorite TV shows, and remind you of all the fun you had watching them. I hope you enjoy it as much as I've enjoyed putting it together!

JJ.

ACKNOWLEDGMENTS:

I owe a great many people a formal "thank you" for their invaluable assistance in putting this book together:

- As always, thanks to Bob Miller, my editor, for his enthusiasm and support. AND for coming up with the title.
- Special citation for performance above and beyond the call of duty: Vicki Rombs, Ed Schilling, Mary Kay Landon, and wonderful Lisa DiMona of St. Martin's.
- Thanks to Connie Boucher and Doug Boucher for their support and forbearance.
- Dave Riggs was an invaluable adviser and cheerleader.
- Thanks to Sharon for making it through another one.
- A tip of the hat to Ron and Roland for their exceptional work. They're two very talented designers.
- Thanks to Gloria Buckles who is one of the NICEST people.
- Thanks to Dodie Randle and Jay Livingston.
- *Mr. Ed* is especially for Harry Trumbore.
- Thanks to Charles Pavlosky at BMI, and Bill Frank at ASCAP for all their research.
- Thanks to Howard Hayes for *I Married Joan*, to Lonnie Graham, Bill Grant, Ira and Cathy Steingroot, Roger Dorfman, and Vern Nelson.
- And finally, my heartfelt thanks to all the people who made the theme songs available: Gay Jones, Arlene Muller, Al Kohn, Jeffrey Beegle, Joan Schulman, Jeff Gordon, Ken Werner, Billie Ward, Lynn Murray, Robin Rosenfeld, Tom Smith, Don Tamsen, Cindy Brown, Richard Trepanier, Sidney Herman, Lewis Bachman, Paul Henning, Jeff Brabec, Joseph Weiss, Maureen Woods, Dan Fisher, Sody Clampett, Dan Hubbert, John Bishop, Mr. Piet, Mr. Kenney, Barbara Brunow.

If I've inadvertently failed to mention anyone who gave me their help, all I can say is "Thanks." It's been a long project, and I really appreciate all the help I received.

Table Of Contents

S it-coms

W esterns

Q uiz show

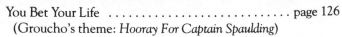

(Groucho's theme: *Hooray For Captain Spaulding*)

Table Of Contents

K ids shows

D rama/action

C ommercials

Green Acres

Eddie Albert played lawyer Oliver Wendell Douglas.

THE SHOW: Oliver Wendell Douglas was a New York lawyer with a fantasy — he wanted to own a farm and have a chance to "feel his hands in the soil." So when Mr. Haney, the country con man, came along with a farm for sale, Oliver snapped it up, sight unseen. That's when his problems began. First, his wife, Lisa, didn't want to leave Manhattan....And when she finally *did*, their farm in Hooterville turned out to be the worst in the county! Add a hapless handyman named Eb Dawson (who called Oliver "Dad"), the Ziffels (whose "son," Arnold, was a pig who watched TV), Mr. Haney (who kept on trying to con Oliver into buying more worthless junk), and dozens of other zany characters, and you had Oliver's "Green Acres dream" — one of the strangest (and funniest) sitcoms on TV.

THE SONG: Written by the author of *The Addams Family* theme, and sung by Eddie Albert and Eva Gabor as they acted it out.

Main Cast

Oliver Wendell Douglas: Eddie Albert
Lisa Douglas (his wife): Eva Gabor
Eb Dawson (the handyman): Tom Lester
Mr. Haney (the con man): Pat Buttram
Hank Kimball (county agent): Alvy Moore
Fred Ziffel (a neighbor): Hank Peterson
Mrs. Ziffel: Fran Ryan, Barbara Pepper
Arnold (a pig): Arnold the Pig

Vital Statistics

Half-hour sitcom. CBS. 170 episodes.
First aired: Sept. 15, 1965
Most popular time slot: Wednesday, 9 – 9:30 PM (1965-68)
Last show: Sept. 7, 1971
Ranked in a year's Top 25: 1966 (11), 1967 (6), 1968 (16), 1969 (19)

INSIDE FACTS

THE ORIGIN OF THE SHOW:

• It was adapted from a radio show called *Granby's Green Acres*, which aired around 1950.
• The show's owner, Jay Sommers, approached the creator of *The Beverly Hillbillies*, Paul Henning, with the idea to turn it into a TV program.
• Enthusiastic, Henning approached CBS executive Jim Aubrey. Aubrey bought the idea without a pilot OR EVEN A SCRIPT! Henning's record was that good.

ABOUT ARNOLD THE PIG:

• There were Arnold fan clubs in colleges all over the country.
• The first Arnold was a male, but all the rest — some 2-4 per year — were females.
• He (she) won two Patsy Awards as Best Animal Actor of the Year.

TRIVIA QUIZ

1. Ralph and Alf were a brother–sister carpenter team who worked on the Douglases' house. Who was the sister?
2. What did the Douglases have to do to make a phone call from their house?
3. What was Eddie Albert's first TV series?
4. What was the Douglases' cow named?
5. Pat Buttram, who played Mr. Haney, was the famous sidekick to a more-famous movie/TV cowboy. Which one?

ANSWERS

5. Gene Autry.
4. Eleanor.
3. Trick question — it was this one.
2. Climb a telephone pole.
1. Ralph.

(OLIVER)
Green Acres is the place for me.
Farm livin' is the life for me.
Land spreadin' out so far and wide
Keep Manhattan, just give me
     the countryside.

(LISA)
New York is where I'd rather stay.
I get allergic smelling hay.
I just adore a penthouse view.
Dah-ling I love you but give me
     Park Avenue

(OLIVER)
. . . . .The chores.

(LISA)
. . . . .The stores.

(OLIVER)
. . . . .Fresh air.

(LISA)
. . . . .Times Square

(OLIVER)
You are my wife.

(LISA)
Good-bye city life.

(TOGETHER)
Green Acres we are there.

7

The Andy Griffith Show

THE SHOW: What do you do on a lazy Saturday afternoon in Mayberry, North Carolina? Grab your fishing pole and amble out to the old fishin' hole. And that's just what Sheriff Andy Taylor and his son Opie did for eight years to open the *Andy Griffith Show*, whistling as they walked. It always seemed like Saturday afternoon in Mayberry. There was plenty of time for Andy to jaw with Floyd and Goober, or drop by for a piece of Aunt Bee's pie. His biggest problem wasn't crime (the only "criminal" in Mayberry was Otis the drunk): it was Deputy Barney Fife, the inept "law in these parts." Fortunately, Andy wouldn't let him keep bullets in his gun. But then, that's how it always was in Mayberry . . . Andy's common sense prevailed, and he never did run out of good advice.

Andy Griffith, 50% owner of one of TV's most successful comedies.

THE SONG: Whistled on the show, but originally written with the lyrics included here.

Main Cast

Andy Taylor (the sheriff): Andy Griffith
Barney Fife (his deputy): Don Knotts
Opie Taylor (his son): Ronnie Howard
Bee Taylor (his aunt): Frances Bavier
Ellie Walker (his girlfriend): Elinor Donahue
Helen Crump (his girlfriend): Anita Corsaut
Gomer Pyle (a gas station attendant): Jim Nabors
Goober Pyle (Gomer's cousin): George Lindsey
Floyd Lawson (the barber): Howard McNair

Vital Statistics

Half-hour sitcom. CBS. 249 episodes.
First aired: Oct. 3, 1960
Time slots: Mon., 9:30 – 10:00 PM (1960-64), 9 – 9:30 PM (1965-68)
Last show: Sept. 16, 1968
Ranked in a year's Top 25: 1961 (4), 1962 (7), 1963 (6), 1964 (5), 1965 (4), 1966 (6), 1967 (3), 1968 (1)

INSIDE FACTS

ABOUT ANDY GRIFFIEH:

• In 1953, at age 27, he recorded a comedy monologue entitled "What It Was, Was Football" for a North Carolina record company.
• A local success, it was bought by Capitol Records, which re-released it on their own label. It became a *national* hit, selling over a million copies.
• Griffith moved on to the lead role in the Broadway *and* movie versions of *No Time For Sergeants*, and was a smash success in both.
• Subsequent films weren't as well received, and offers for new roles fell off — so Griffith decided to find a TV series.
• The pilot of *The Andy Griffith Show* was aired as an episode of *The Danny Thomas Show* in 1959. Griffith played a small-town mayor, and sponsors signed him for a series immediately.

TRIVIA QUIZ

1. Which *Andy Griffith* regular starred as an alien being named Fum in a mid-'70s TV series called *The Lost Saucer*?
2. Elinor Donahue, Andy's long-time girl friend, was "Princess" for 9 years on which sitcom?
3. Where did Barney keep his bullet?
4. Who took over as Mayberry's #1 citizen when Andy left?
5. What was Andy's relationship to Barney?

ANSWERS

1. Jim Nabors.
2. *Father Knows Best.*
3. In his shirt pocket.
4. Ken Berry.
5. Barney was his cousin.

"The Andy Griffith Show" (The Fishin' Hole)

Lyrics: Everett Sloane, Music: Earle Hagen, Herbert Spencer

9

Wheth – er it's hot,   Wheth – er it's
Hang – in' a— round,   Tak – in' our

cool,   Oh — what a spot.   for
ease,   Watch – in' that hound,   a—

10

whist – lin' like a fool.   What a   fine   day to
scratch – in' at his fleas. Come on, take   down your

take a stroll and wan –der by The Fish–in' Hole, I can't think of a
fish – in' pole and meet me at The Fish–in' Hole, I can't think of a

bet–ter way to pass the time o'day. —   2. We'll have
bet-   to pass the time o'day. —

The Beverly Hillbillies

THE SHOW: The most popular show on TV in its first season, it became the most popular series in *history* by its second. The premise was simple: Jed Clampett, an impoverished Ozark hillbilly, went hunting one day and found oil on his land — $25,000,000 worth. So he and his family piled into their 1921 Oldsmobile truck and moved to a Beverly Hills mansion, right next door to the Drysdales. But location is about *all* they changed. They kept the truck and their old clothes; Granny kept making "potions" and cooking possum-bellies; Elly May filled the place up with "critters"; and Jethro never did figure out why someone always showed up at the door when a bell rang. They drove Mrs. Drysdale crazy. "But this is Beverly Hills," she wailed in one episode. "Dirt is dirt," replied Granny.

THE SONG: Written by the show's creator and producer, Paul Henning, and recorded by Flatt and Scruggs, a bluegrass duo. It hit #44 on the charts in 1962.

Y'all come back, now . . . Hear?

Main Cast

Jed Clampett: Buddy Ebsen
Granny (his mother-in-law): Irene Ryan
Elly May (his daughter): Donna Douglas
Jethro Bodine (his nephew): Max Baer
Milburn Drysdale (the banker): Raymond Bailey
Margaret Drysdale (his wife): Harriet MacGibbon
Jane Hathaway (his secretary): Nancy Kulp

Vital Statistics

Half-hour sitcom. CBS.
First aired: Sept. 26, 1962
Most popular time slot: Wednesday, 8:30 – 9:00 PM (1964-68, 69-70)
Last show: Sept. 7, 1971
Ranked in a year's Top 25: 1963 (1), 1964 (1), 1965 (12), 1966 (8), 1967 (9), 1968 (12), 1969 (10), 1970 (18)

INSIDE FACTS

THE SHOW'S CREATOR:
• Paul Henning created, produced, and wrote the series.
• Previously he had been a writer on *The Fibber McGee and Molly* radio show, and produced *The Dennis Day Show* and *Love That Bob* for television.
• He also developed *Petticoat Junction* and *Green Acres*, two of the 1960s' most popular shows.

ABOUT BUDDY EBSEN:
• He was originally a dancer, beginning is career as his sister's dance partner in 1928.
• He was the original choice for the role of The Tin Man in the MGM film, *The Wizard of Oz*, but had to withdraw from it when he suffered a collapsed lung from inhaling metal dust in the costume.

TRIVIA QUIZ

1. What was the name of Mr. Drysdale's bank?
2. What was the "double-barrelled sling-shot"?
3. What was the "see-ment pond"?
4. What was the Clampetts' bloodhound's name?
5. Who played Jethro's sister, Jethrine?

ANSWERS
1. The Commerce Bank of Beverly Hills.
2. A bra, adapted by Elly May.
3. The Clampetts swimming pool.
4. Duke.
5. Max Baer, Jr. in drag. The voice was supplied by Linda Kaye Henning.

Ballad of Jed Clampett

Lyrics and Music: Paul Henning

1. Come 'n lis — ten to my stor — ry 'bout a man name Jed _____
2. Well, the first thing you know, Ol' Jed's a mil — lion — aire _____
3. Ol' _____ Jed bought a man — sion, Law — dy, it was swank _____
4. Well, _____ now it's time to say good bye to Jed and all his kin _____ an'

Poor moun tain eer, bare — ly kept his fam' — ly fed. An'
Kin — folk _____ said, "Jed, _____ move a — way from there". Said,
Next door _____ neigh — bor was pres — 'dent of the bank. Lotsa
they would like t' thank you folks fer kind — ly drop — pin' — in. You're

Then one day, he was shoot — in' at some food, an'
"Cal — i — for — ny is th' place y' ought — a be, so, they
Folks ob — ject — ed, but the bank — er found no fault, 'cause
All in — vit — ed back a — gain to this lo — cal — i ty t'

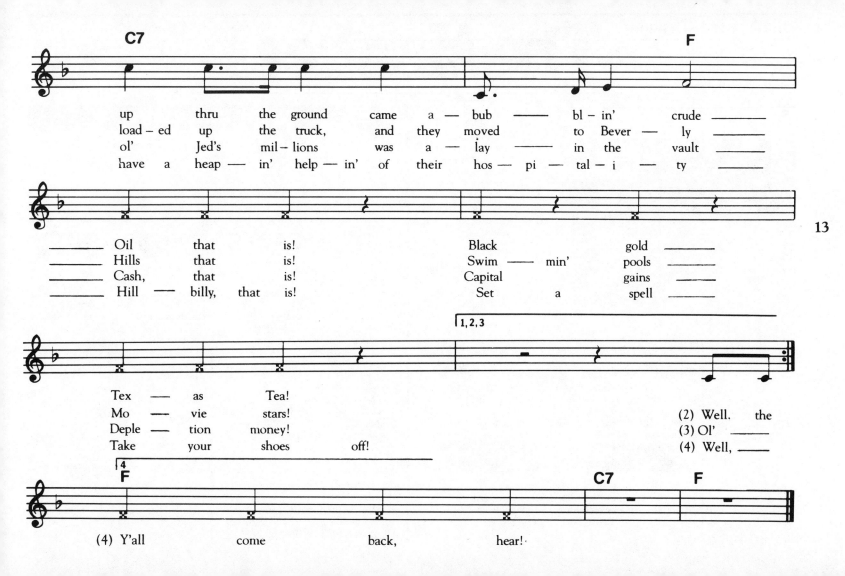

13

The Monkees

THE SHOW: "Hey, Hey! It's the Monkees!" Inspired by the Beatles' film, *A Hard Day's Night*, Don Kirshner created this show about the exploits of a zany rock'n'roll quartet. The Monkees — Mickey, Mike, Davy, and Peter (everyone had a favorite) — were basically clean-cut, nice guys who always tried to help people (proving that the younger generation — long hair and all — wasn't so bad). But somehow, they always wound up in trouble themselves. And that invariably led to the weekly chase, with the Monkees running upside down, backwards, speeded-up, extra slow — anything but normal. In the end, the foursome always saved the fair damsel, caught the crooks (usually in spite of themselves), and then celebrated by playing a song off their latest album. With prime time support, they had 11 hits in less than two years. But the Monkees were a short-lived phenomenon, and the hits ended when the show was cancelled in 1968.

THE SONG: Sung by the Monkees, it was written by prolific rock songwriters Boyce and Hart.

Mickey Dolenz, singing lead at a Monkees concert.

Main Cast

Davy Jones: Davy Jones
Michael Nesmith: Michael Nesmith
Mickey Dolenz: Mickey Dolenz
Peter Tork: Peter Tork

Vital Statistics

Half-hour sitcom. NBC. 58 episodes.
First aired: Sept. 12, 1966
Time slot: Monday, 7:30 – 8:00 PM (1966-68)
Last show: Aug. 19, 1968
Never ranked in the Top 25 shows of a year.

INSIDE FACTS

MISCELLANEOUS:
● To cast *The Monkees*, the show's producers placed an ad in *Variety* magazine.
● 437 aspiring rock stars answered it and were interviewed by *The Monkees'* producers before they came up with the final four.
● After being selected, the four had to take a six week course in improvisational acting.
● Steve Stills, who became a rock superstar with Buffalo Springfield and Crosby, Stills, and Nash, auditioned for *The Monkees* and was turned down.
● Davy Jones, an ex-jockey from Manchester, England, was the only group-member who was not picked through the ad.
● Mickey Dolenz had been the star of *Circus Boy*, 1956-58, using the name Mickey Braddock.

TRIVIA QUIZ

1. Which Monkee had been a Mouseketeer?
2. Which Monkee wrote Linda Ronstadt's hit, *Different Drum*?
3. The Monkees had the #1 song of 1967. What was it?
4. Which Monkee's father was a Washington, D.C. college professor?
5. The Monkees had two million-sellers in 1966. Name one.

ANSWERS

1. Mickey Dolenz.
2. Mike Nesmith.
3. *Daydream Believer.*
4. Peter Tork.
5. *Last Train to Clarksville*, and *I'm A Believer.*

(Theme from) **The Monkees**

by Tommy Boyce and Bobby Hart

Here we come,
Walkin' down the street,
We get the funniest looks from
Ev'ryone we meet.

Chorus:
Hey, hey we're the Monkees,
and people say we monkey around.
But we're too busy singing
To put anybody down.

We go wherever we want to,
Do what we like to do.
We don't have time to get restless,
There's always something new.

CHORUS

Any time,
Or anywhere
Just look over your shoulder,
Guess who's standing there.

CHORUS

We're just tryin' to be friendly,
Come watch us sing and play.
We're the young generation,
And we got something to say.

Hey, hey we're the Monkees,
You never know where we'll be found.
So you'd better get ready,
We may be comin' to your town.

Hey, hey we're the Monkees.

Laverne and Shirley

Talented comedienne Penny Marshall, played Laverne.

THE SHOW: 1950s Milwaukee was the setting of *Happy Days*, and its spinoff series, *Laverne and Shirley*. Both shows were about teenagers, but there was a class difference. In the white-collar *Happy Days*, Richie went to college after high school; in its blue-collar spinoff, Laverne DeFazio and her best friend Shirley Feeney, went to work in the bottle-capping division of the Shotz Brewery. They got their own apartment, too, so they could do whatever they wanted. Except that this was the '50s, and girls didn't *do* what they wanted. Well, maybe Laverne. But not Shirley... never in a zillion years! In fact, the only regular male visitors the girls had were Lenny and Squiggy, a pair of half-wit neighbors who looked like refugees from a Munsters cast party. Some fun, huh? Anyway, Laverne was a still a friend of Fonzie's.

THE SONG: A national hit for Cyndi Grecco in 1976 Run down the street with a friend while you sing it.

Main Cast

Laverne DeFazio: Penny Marshall
Shirley Feeney: Cindy Williams
Lenny Kosnowski (a neighbor): Michael McKean
Squiggy Squiggman (a neighbor): David Lander
Frank DeFazio (Laverne's father): Betty Garrett
Carmine Ragusa (a friend): Eddie Mekka
Edna Babbish (the landlady): Betty Garrett

Vital Statistics

Half-hour sitcom. ABC. 178 episodes.
First aired: Jan. 27th, 1976
Most popular time slot: Tuesday, 8:30 PM (Jan. 1976-July 1979)
Last show: May 3, 1983
Ranked in a year's Top 25: 1976 (3), 1977 (2), 1978 (1), 1979 (1), 1981 (21), 1982 (21)

INSIDE FACTS

ABOUT THE STARS:
• Penny Marshall was the sister of the show's creator and Executive Producer, Garry Marshall.
• She had been a regular on *The Odd Couple*, and a semi-regular on the *Bob Newhart* and *Mary Tyler Moore* shows.
• Cindy Williams starred in *American Grafitti* as Ron Howard's girl friend.
• In 1976, she walked out of the show, upset that Laverne was getting all the good lines. She returned two days later.
• David Lander and Michael McKean were originally hired as writers/consultants.
• They wrote themselves into the show as Squiggy and Lenny — two characters they had created in college in 1966.

TRIVIA QUIZ

1. What did Carmine, the "Big Ragoo," do for a living?
2. What was the name of Laverne's father's business?
3. What was Shirley's good luck charm?
4. What was Squiggy's "real" first name?
5. Michael McKean (Lenny) starred in what popular 1984 movie?

ANSWERS

1. He was a dance instructor.
2. The Pizza bowl, a combination pizza parlor/bowling alley.
3. Boo-Boo Kitty, a cloth cat.
4. Andrew.
5. *This Is Spinal Tap.*

Making Our Dreams Come True

Lyrics: Norman Gimbel, Music: Charles Fox

One two three four five six seven eight.
Shlemeel, shlemazel,
hasenfeffer incorporated.

We're gonna do it!

Give us any chance, we'll take it.
Read us any rule, we'll break it.
We're gonna make our dreams come true,
Doin' it our way.

Nothin's gonna turn us back now,
Straight ahead and on the track now.
We're gonna make our dreams come true,
Doin' it our way.

There is nothing we won't try;
Never heard the word impossible.
This time there's no stopping us.
We're gonna do it.

17

On your mark get set and go now.
Got a dream and we just know now,
We're gonna make that dream come true,
And we'll do it our way, yes our way.
Make all our dreams come true,
And do it our way, yes our way,
Make all our dreams come true
For me and you.

Leave It To Beaver

THE SHOW: In the '50s, the Cleavers were television's image of what an All-American family ought to be. Beaver was a seven-year-old who called adults "sir" and "ma'am" and always got into "just enough" trouble; his father, Ward, was an accountant who always wore a shirt and tie (even at home); his mother, June, was always either cleaning the house (wearing high heels and a dress) or serving Beaver milk and cookies as a solution to his problems. And if milk and cookies didn't work, then Beaver had to take his problems to Wally, his older and wiser brother (who was

Jerry Mathers and Tony Dow, the stars of Leave It To Beaver.

twelve). Wally's solution was to throw a pillow at Beaver. The kids' friends — Lumpy, Larry, and Whitey — were just as "typical". All except the legendary Eddie Haskell, whose most memorable trait was an ability to talk out of both sides of his mouth at once.

THE SONG: Adapted as an instrumental for the theme, it was originally a tune about a parade of toys!

Main Cast

Beaver Cleaver: Jerry Mathers
Ward Cleaver (his father): Hugh Beaumont
June Cleaver (his mother): Barbara Billingsly
Wally Cleaver (his brother): Tony Dow
Eddie Haskell (Wally's pal): Ken Osmond
"Lumpy" Rutherford (Wally's pal): Frank Bank
Larry Mondello (Beaver's pal): Rusty Stevens
Fred Rutherford (Lumpy's father): Richard Deacon

Vital Statistics

Half-hour sitcom. CBS (1957-58), ABC (1958-63). 234 episodes.
First aired: Oct. 4, 1957
Most popular time slot: Saturday, 8:30 – 9:00 PM (1959-62)
Last show: Sept. 12, 1963
Never ranked in the Top 25 shows of a year.

INSIDE FACTS

ABOUT THE STARS:

• Jerry Mathers was "discovered" at age 2 by a department store manager who used his photo on the store's Xmas calendar.

• At age 2½, Mathers made his TV debut on *The Ed Wynn Show* (1954).

• In 1955, he acted in his first movie — Alfred Hitchcock's *The Trouble With Harry*. He appeared in two more films before *Leave It To Beaver* premiered in 1957.

• Tony Dow was the son of an *Our Gang* star.

• He got into acting accidentally, accompanying a friend to an audition for moral support. But he was hired instead of his friend.

• Barbara Billingsley was convinced that she got the part of June Cleaver because "the producers felt sorry for her."

TRIVIA QUIZ

1. On what kind of cereal box did Jerry Mathers and Tony Dow appear?

2. What was the Cleavers' address?

3. In real life, what did Eddie Haskell (Ken Osmond) grow up to be?

4. What was the name of Beaver's elementary school?

5. In what sports was Tony Dow a champion?

ANSWERS

1. Kellogg's Corn Flakes.
2. 211 Pine Street, Mayfield.
3. A police officer.
4. Grant Ave. Elementary School.
5. Swimming and diving.

"Leave It To Beaver" (The Toy Parade)

Lyrics and Music: Dave Kahn, Melvyn Leonard, Mort Greene

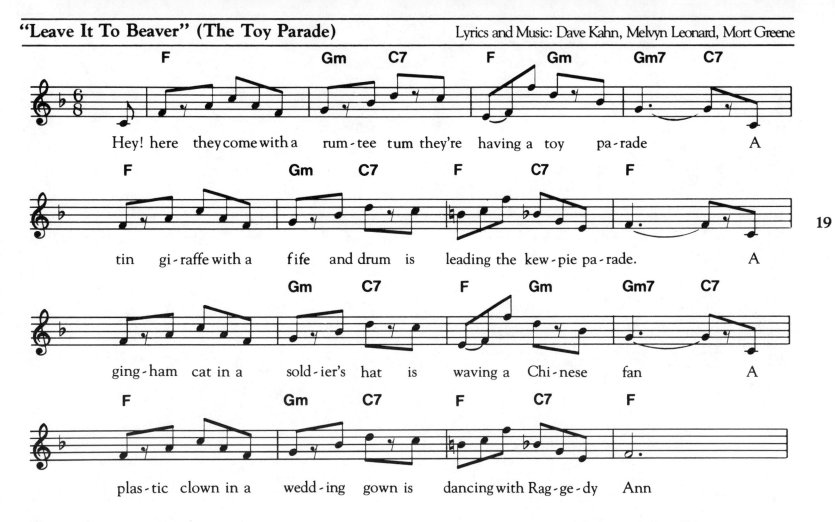

Hey! here they come with a rum-tee tum they're having a toy pa-rade A

tin gi-raffe with a fife and drum is leading the kew-pie pa-rade. A

ging-ham cat in a sold-ier's hat is waving a Chi-nese fan A

plas-tic clown in a wedd-ing gown is dancing with Rag-ge-dy Ann

19

The Many Loves of Dobie Gillis

Dobie Gillis was based on a novel by Max Schulman, author of *Rally 'Round the Flag, Boys,* and *The Tender Trap.* It was a cult show among teenagers, who identified with its heroes: Dobie, a confused, girl-crazy high school student perpetually at war with his father ("I've gotta kill that kid!"), and TV's first sitcom beatnik, Maynard G. Krebs ("You rang?"), who was so averse to work ("WORK!") that the mention of the word would start him shaking. Dobie's heart-throb was Thalia, a beautiful golddigger whose only goal was "oodles and oodles" of money; his nemeses were Chatworth, a boorish snob whose wealth got him everything Dobie dreamed of, and Zelda ("Hi, Poopsie"), a homely girl determined to marry Dobie. His father waited in vain for him to "come to his senses" and take over the Gillis Grocery Store, but Dobie was after bigger things. The problem was, he never could figure out what.

Dwayne Hickman starred as Dobie Gillis

Main Cast

Dobie: Dwayne Hickman
Herbert T. Gillis (his father): Frank Faylen
Winnie Gillis (his mother): Florida Friebus
Maynard G. Krebs (his pal): Bob Denver
Thalia Meninger (the beauty): Tuesday Weld
Zelda Gilroy (his pursuer): Sheila James
Chatsworth Osborne, Jr. (the snob): Steve Franken
Mr. Pomfritt (teacher): William Schallert
Mrs. Adams/Dr. Burkhart (teacher): Jean Byron

Vital Statistics

Half-hour sitcom. CBS. 147 episodes.
First aired: Sept. 29, 1959
Most popular time slot: Tuesday, 8:30 – 9:00 PM (1959-62)
Last show: Sept. 18, 1963
Ranked in a year's Top 25: 1961 (23), 1962 (22)

INSIDE FACTS

ABOUT THE STARS:

• Dwayne Hickman starred as Robert Cummings' nephew in *Love That Bob* from 1955-58.
• He never starred in another series, but went on to become an executive at CBS.
• 23-year-old Bob Denver was working the night shift at a post office during Christmas, 1958, when he was asked to an early-morning audition for the role of Maynard. Not having slept, he was so haggard that he looked too old for the part. But the next day he returned (after a night's sleep), and won the role.
• He went on to play Gilligan, in *Gilligan's Island,* and Dusty, in *Dusty's Trails.*

TRIVIA QUIZ

1. What did Maynard call Dobie?
2. What did Chatsworth call Dobie?
3. Dobie delivered his weekly monologue in front of which statue?
4. How did Zelda say she knew that Dobie loved her?
5. Florida Friebus, Dobie's mom, was a regular group therapy patient in what '70s series?

ANSWERS

1. "Good Buddy".
2. "Dobie – do".
3. Rodin's "The Thinker".
4. She wrinkled up her nose, and he involuntarily did it back.
5. *The Bob Newhart Show.*

Dobie

Words: Max Shulman, Music: Lionel Newman

DO-BIE   wants a lit-tle cu-tie,   DO-BIE

wants a lit-tle beau-ty;   DO-BIE   wants a gal to call his own.

An- y size, an- y style, an- y

eyes, an- y smile, An- y Jean, an- y Jane, an- y Joan.   Oh,

DO-BIE wants a girl who's dream-y, DO-BIE wants a girl who's cream-y,

DO-BIE wants a girl to call his own. Is she

23

blond, is she tall, is she dark, is she small, Is she an-y kind-a dream-boat at all;

No mat-ter, He's hers and hers a-lone.

The Brady Bunch

THE SHOW: Michael Brady, a Los Angeles architect and a widower with three boys, met Carol Martin, a widow with three girls. They fell in love, got married, and crammed their whole family into a four-bedroom, two-bathroom house on Clinton Avenue. If it wasn't already crowded enough, they also had a cat, a dog named Tiger, and a live-in housekeeper named Alice (where did *she* sleep?). That was the premise for this popular comedy, which concerned itself exclusively with everyday problems like doing the dishes, hogging the bathroom, getting to school on time, etc.

Robert Reed and Florence Henderson, "parents" of the Brady Bunch

And the family had enormous appeal; *The Brady Bunch* was resurrected three times in the next 10 years — as a cartoon, as a "return of", and as *The Brady Brides*.

THE SONG: Co-written by Sherwood Schwartz, the show's creator and Executive Producer, and sung by the cast.

Main Cast

Carol Brady (the mother): Florence Henderson
Mike Brady (the father): Robert Reed
Alice Nelson (the housekeeper): Ann B. Davis
Marcia Brady (a daughter): Maureen McCormick
Janis Brady (a daughter): Eve Plumb
Cindy Brady (a daughter): Susan Olsen
Peter Brady (a son): Christopher Knight
Greg Brady (a son): Barry Williams
Bobby Brady (a son): Michael Lookinland

Vital Statistics

Half-hour sitcom. ABC. 117 episodes.
First aired: Sept. 26, 1969
Most popular time slot: Friday, 8 – 8:30 PM (1969-70, 1971-74)
Last show: Aug. 30, 1974
Never ranked in the Top 25 shows of a year.

INSIDE FACTS

ABOUT THE BRADY KIDS:

• Executive Producer Sherwood Schwartz interviewed 464 girls and boys to find the right Brady kids.
• He hadn't picked the adult leads yet, but knew he wanted the kids to have the same color hair as their "parents."
• His solution: he picked two sets of Brady boys, two sets of Brady girls: (blonde and brunette).
• When Reed and Henderson were chosen, Schwartz dropped the blonde boys and brunette girls.
• The most popular Brady kid was Barry Williams, who became an instant pop star, getting 6500 letters per week in 1971.
• The stand-ins for the Brady kids were a middle-aged midget couple.

TRIVIA QUIZ

1. Robert Reed's first regular series was an Emmy Award-winning lawyer show in the early '60s. Name it.
2. The youngest Brady kid claimed to have retired from show business at age three, and made a comeback at age five. Which one was she?
3. Which Brady cast member got her start in show biz as a Baby Miss San Fernando Valley?
4. Ann B. Davis starred as "Schultzy" in what popular '50s sitcom?
5. Which Brady girl didn't return for the *Brady Brides*?

ANSWERS:

1. *The Defenders.*
2. Cindy, Susan Olsen.
3. Marcia, Maureen McCormick.
4. *Love That Bob.*
5. Janis, Eve Plumb.

Here's the story of a lovely lady
Who was bringing up three very lovely girls.
All of them had hair of gold
   like their mother,
The youngest one in curls.

It's the story of a man named Brady,
Who was busy with three boys of his own.
They were four men living all together,
Yet they were all alone.

Till the one day when the lady
   met this fellow,
And they knew it was much more than
   a hunch,
That this group should somehow form
   a family.
That's the way we all became the
   Brady Bunch,
The Brady Bunch,
That's the way we all became the
   Brady Bunch.

The Brady Bunch.

25

All In The Family

THE SHOW: Archie and Edith Bunker lived in New York with their daughter Gloria and their son-in-law, a college student named Mike Stivic (whom Archie called "Meathead"). Edith (Archie called *her* "Dingbat") was a dimwitted but compassionate woman. Archie, who worked as a dock foreman for the Prendergast Tool and Die Company, was anything *but* compassionate; he was opinionated, abusive, pushy and bigoted. His conversation was sprinkled with terms like "jungle bunny," "Hebe," "Spic," and "Wop" — but somehow he wasn't offensive — he was funny! It took a program as well-written and perfectly casted as *All In The Family* to bring the real world to sitcoms.

A legend in his own time, Carroll O'Connor played Archie Bunker, America's favorite bigot.

THE SONG: Sung over the opening credits by Archie and Edith, as Edith played the piano. Its title was the program's original name; it has some of the best theme song lyrics ever.

Main Cast

Archie Bunker: Carroll O'Connor
Edith Bunker (his wife): Jean Stapleton
Gloria Stivic (his daughter): Sally Struthers
Mike Stivic (his son-in-law): Rob Reiner
Stephanie Mills (a niece): Danielle Brisebois
Teresa Betancourt (a boarder): Liz Torres
Bert Munson (a friend): Billy Halop
The Jeffersons (neighbors): see page 36

Vital Statistics

Half-hour sitcom. CBS.
First aired: Jan. 12, 1971
Most popular time slot: Saturday, 8 – 8:30 PM (1971-75)
Last show: Sept. 9, 1979
Ranked in a year's Top 25: 1972 (1), 1973 (1), 1974 (1), 1975 (1), 1976 (1), 1977 (12), 1978 (6), 1979 (9)

INSIDE FACTS

ABOUT THE SHOW'S ORIGIN:

• It was inspired by *Til Death Do Us Part*, an English sitcom that portrayed a working-class family.
• Norman Lear read about the show in 1968, and bought the American rights to it.
• He wrote a script for a pilot film, "Americanizing" the show, and sold the concept to ABC.
• He made two pilots for ABC (calling the show *Those Were The Days*), but they eventually shelved the whole project and forgot about it.
• A year later, CBS called Lear and asked to see the pilot.
• They loved it, and promised to get it on the air in the first available time slot.

TRIVIA QUIZ

NAME THE CHARACTER OR CAST MEMBER WHO:
1. In 1974, refused to cross a picket line, forcing a change in the shooting schedule.
2. Was the son of the creator of the *Dick Van Dyke Show*.
3. Was going to be murdered while at a convention (on the show) if contract re-negotiations with the actor who played him weren't successful.
4. Inspired a religious book describing her Christianity.
5. Sued to get out of her contract in 1974.

ANSWERS:
1. Carroll O'Connor
2. Rob Reiner
3. Archie Bunker
4. Edith Bunker
5. Sally Struthers

Boy the way Glenn Miller played
Songs that made the hit parade.
Guys like me we had it made,
Those Were The Days.

Didn't need no welfare state,
Everybody pulled his weight,
Gee our old LaSalle ran great,
Those Were The Days.

And you knew who you were then,
Girls were girls and men were men.
Mister we could use a man
Like Herbert Hoover again.

People seemed to be content,
Fifty dollars paid the rent,
Freaks were in a circus tent,
Those Were The Days.

Take a little Sunday spin,
Go and watch the Dodgers win,
Have yourself a dandy day,
that cost you under a fin.

Hair was short and skirts were long,
Kate Smith really sold a song,
I don't know just what went wrong,
Those Were The Days.

27

A Song From A Sponsor

See the U.S.A. In Your Chevrolet

Written by Leon Carr and Leo Corday

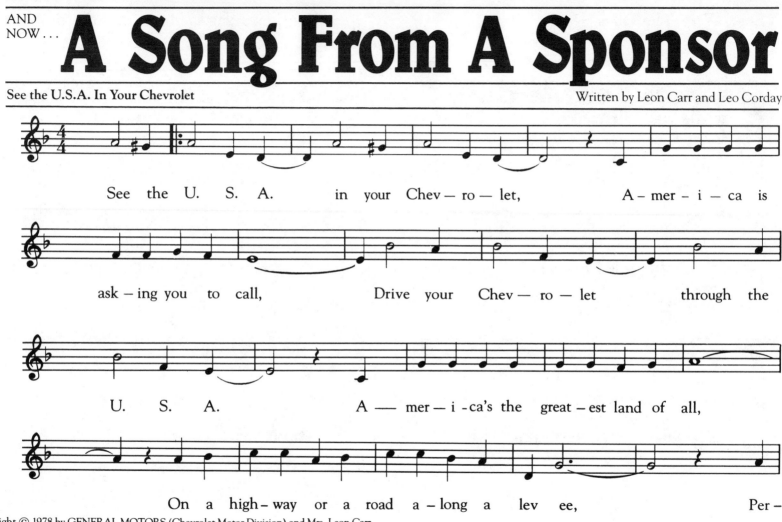

See the U. S. A. in your Chev — ro — let, A — mer — i — ca is

28

ask – ing you to call, Drive your Chev — ro — let through the

U. S. A. A — mer — i — ca's the great — est land of all,

On a high – way or a road a – long a lev ee, Per –

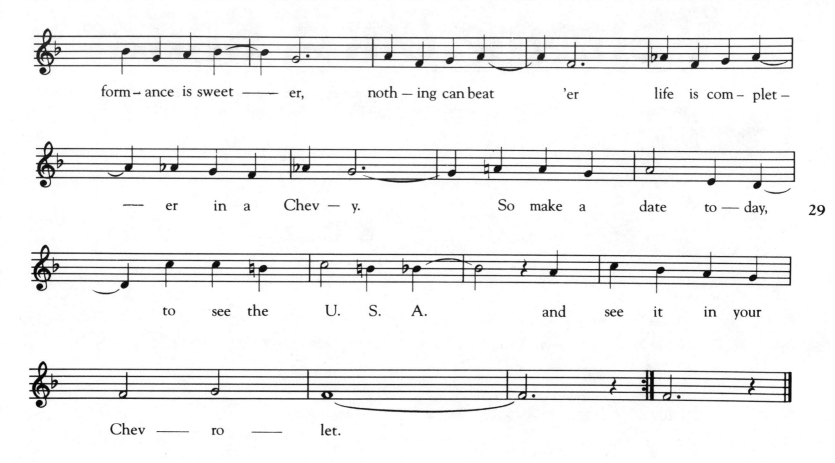

form – ance is sweet —— er,   noth – ing can beat   'er   life is com – plet –

—— er in a   Chev — y.   So make a   date   to — day,   29

to   see the   U.   S.   A.   and   see   it   in your

Chev —— ro —— let.

Welcome Back, Kotter

THE SHOW: Gabe Kotter, once a problem student, returned to his alma mater — James Buchanan High School — as a teacher. His class: a group of "unteachable" misfits and cut-ups called the Sweathogs (led by John Travolta as Vinnie Barbarino, in the role that made him a star). "Mr. Kot-tair" was clearly the only teacher who had ever been able to reach them — or who even cared enough to try — and a warm friendship soon developed. They frequently visited him and his wife Julie at home, and when she gave birth to twin girls, they were on hand to help out. Prowling around: cranky Vice Principal Woodman, doing his best to get the Sweathogs thrown out of school.

Gabe Kaplan, aka Gabe Kotter

THE SONG: Written by John Sebastian, leader of the Lovin' Spoonful in the '60s, who also wrote *Daydream, Do You Believe In Magic*, etc. It was the only TV theme *ever* to hit #1, selling more than a million copies in 1976.

Main Cast

Gabe Kotter (the teacher): Gabe Kaplan
Julie Kotter (his wife): Marcia Strassman
Mr. Woodman (Vice-principal): John S. White
The Sweathogs
Vinnie Barbarino: John Travolta
Juan Epstien: Robert Hegyes
Freddie Washington: Lawrence-Hilton Jacobs
Arnold Horshack: Ron Palillo
Beau De Labarre: Stephen Shortridge

Vital Statistics

Half-hour sitcom. ABC.
First aired: Sept. 9, 1975
Most popular time slot: Thursday, 8 – 8:30 PM (Jan. '76-Aug. '78)
Last show: Aug. 10, 1979
Ranked in a year's Top 25: 1976 (18), 1977 (13)

INSIDE FACTS

MISCELLANEOUS:

• Like Kotter, Gabe Kaplan came from the inner city, in Brooklyn.
• He dropped out of high school to become a minor league baseball player, but couldn't run fast enough to get on a team.
• Instead, he became a standup comedian.
• In 1974, a TV producer saw and liked his act, and the two of them came up with the idea for *Kotter* over dinner soon after.
• The National Education Assoc. wanted a "technical adviser" on *Kotter*'s set "to protect the image of school teachers."
• Kaplan's answer: "Would you believe a technical adviser on the set of *Sanford and Son* to protect the image of junk dealers?"

TRIVIA QUIZ

THE SUBJECT IS ... TEACHERS

Kotter was one of many TV school teachers. How many of these TV teachers can you name?
1. A handsome high school teacher played by James Franciscus.
2. He was called the White Shadow.
3. Bill Cosby played this high school gym teacher on *The Bill Cosby Show*.
4. The law professor on *Paper Chase*, played by John Housman.
5. Lloyd Haynes played this history teacher on *Room 222*.

ANSWERS

1. Mr. Novak
2. Ken Reeves
3. Chet Kincaid
4. Charles Kingsfield, Jr.
5. Pete Dixon

Welcome Back Kotter

Lyrics and Music: John Sebastian

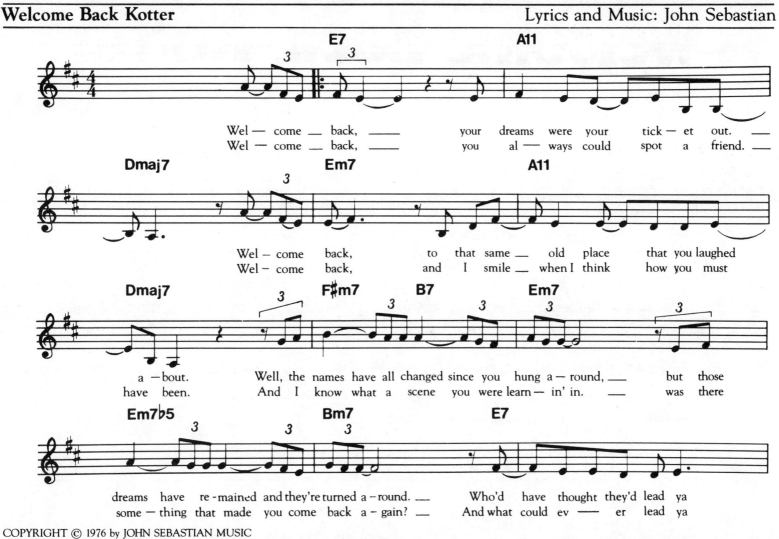

Wel — come — back, _____ your dreams were your tick — et out. _____
Wel — come — back, _____ you al — ways could spot a friend. _____

Wel — come — back, to that same _____ old place that you laughed
Wel — come — back, and I smile _____ when I think how you must

a —bout. Well, the names have all changed since you hung a — round, _____ but those
have been. And I know what a scene you were learn — in' in. _____ was there

dreams have re —mained and they're turned a —round. _____ Who'd have thought they'd lead ya
some — thing that made you come back a —gain? _____ And what could ev — — er lead ya

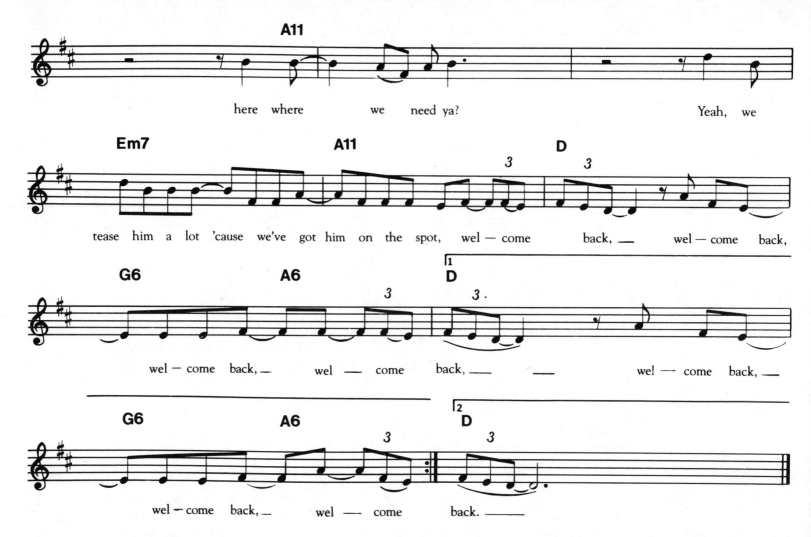

here where   we   need ya?   Yeah,   we

32

tease   him   a   lot   'cause   we've   got   him   on   the   spot,   wel — come   back, __   wel — come   back,

wel — come   back, __   wel — come   back, __   __   wel — come   back, __

wel — come   back, __   wel — come   back. _____

Mr. Ed

THE SHOW: When architect Wilbur Post and his wife Carol moved to their new home in the country, they made a surprising discovery: the previous owners had left them a horse — a palomino named Mr. Ed. Wilbur took an immediate liking to him. Then one day, while Wilbur was brushing Mr. Ed down, he made another discovery: Mr. Ed talked! AND Mr. Ed would only talk to HIM! They became good friends, and Wilbur spent the rest of the series keeping Ed out of trouble while he tried to keep his talking horse a secret. "Wee-il-burr!"

Mr. Ed does the town.

THE SONG: Sung by Jay Livingston, one of its composers (and *Bonanza*'s). The music for the pilot was done in Italy, but the Italians who were scoring the theme originally chose an opera singer for the song. He sang it so poorly that the show's producers were going to drop it altogether...until Livingston offered HIS version, which is the one we all know and love.

Main Cast

Wilbur Post (an architect): Alan Young
Carol Post (his wife): Connie Hines
Roger Addison (a neighbor): Larry Keating
Kay Addison (his wife): Edna Skinner
Gordon Kirkwood (a neighbor): Leon Ames
Winnie Kirkwood (his wife): Florence MacMichael
Mr. Carlisle (Carol's dad): Barry Kelly
Ed's voice: Allan "Rocky" Lane

Vital Statistics

Half-hour sitcom. CBS. 143 episodes.
First aired: Oct. 1, 1961
Most popular time slot: Sunday, 6:30 – 7:00 PM (1961-62, 1963-64)
Last show: Sept. 8, 1965
Never ranked in a year's Top 25 shows.

INSIDE FACTS

ABOUT MR. ED:

• The character originated in a series of magazine stories in which the horse not only talked, but got drunk.
• The palomino was born in 1946, and died Feb. 28, 1979. He was 33 years old.
• They made the horse look like he was talking by putting a piece of nylon mesh under his top lip. He was really trying to dislodge it.
• The man who supplied Mr. Ed's voice was a 1930s cowboy movie star.

ABOUT ALAN YOUNG:

• In the early '50s, he had his own TV show, and was considered a major up-and-coming star.
• *TV Guide* called him "the Charlie Chaplin of Television" in 1952.

TRIVIA QUIZ

1. Mr. Ed's producer also directed a series of movies in the '40s about a talking mule named _____.
2. CBS had another horse show from 1956 to 1958. It was called *My Friend* _____.
3. Why would Ed only talk to Wilbur?
4. Richard Deacon, Dr. Bruce Gordon on Mr. Ed, is famous for his role on *The Dick Van Dyke Show*. What was it?
5. Stumper: what was the real name of the horse who played Mr. Ed?

ANSWERS

5. Bamboo Harvester.
4. Mel Cooley.
3. He was the first person Mr. Ed had met who was worth talking to.
2. Flicka.
1. Francis.

33

Mister Ed

Lyrics and Music by Jay Livingston and Ray Evans

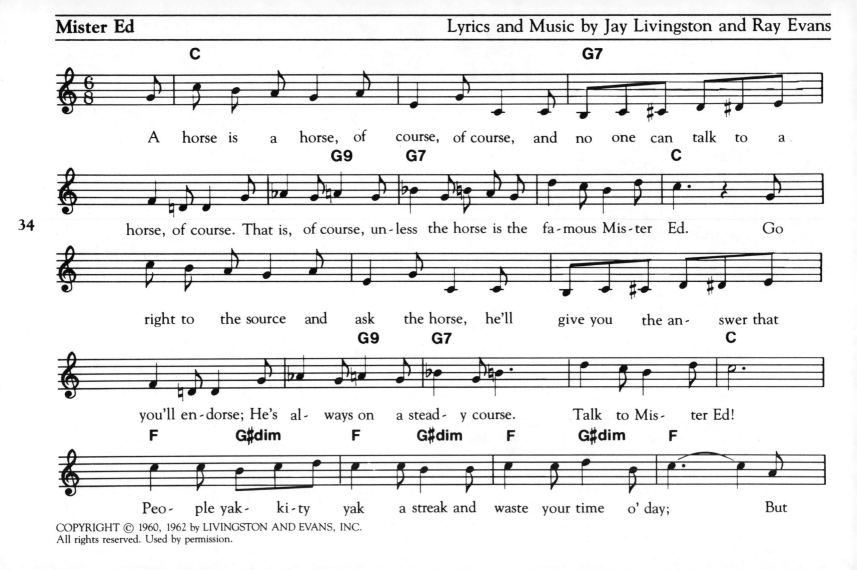

A horse is a horse, of course, of course, and no one can talk to a horse, of course. That is, of course, un-less the horse is the fa-mous Mis-ter Ed. Go right to the source and ask the horse, he'll give you the an- swer that you'll en-dorse; He's al- ways on a stead- y course. Talk to Mis- ter Ed! Peo- ple yak- ki-ty yak a streak and waste your time o' day; But

34

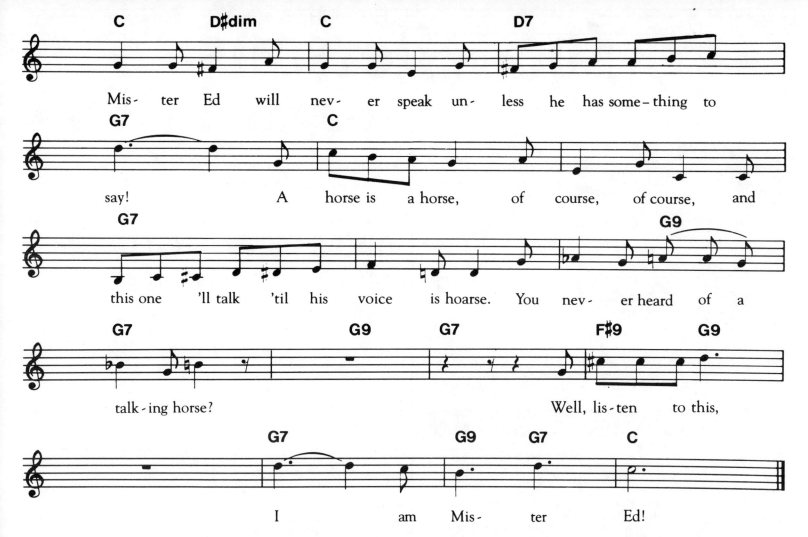

The Jeffersons

THE SHOW: America was introduced to blustery George Jefferson's family on *All In The Family*, as the Bunkers' next door neighbors. Louise was Edith's good friend; Lionel and Mike were friends; but George and Archie couldn't stand each other, probably because they were so much alike — loud, obnoxious, domineering, and bigoted. Soon George's dry cleaning shop grew into a small chain, so the Jeffersons "moved on up" to a fancy apartment in Manhattan's upper east side ... *and* their own series. The new Jefferson household included Florence, the wise-cracking maid, and occasionally Mother Jefferson. New neighbors: Tom and Helen Willis, TV sitcoms' first inter-racial couple, their daughter Jenny (later Lionel's bride), and a goofy U.N. translator named Harry Bentley.

THE SONG: A Gospel song about getting rich. Clap your hands, brothers and sisters, and praise capitalism!

Sherman Hemsley, star of The Jeffersons.

Main Cast

George Jefferson: Sherman Hemsley
Louise Jefferson: Isabel Sanford
Lionel Jefferson (their son): Mike Evans, Damon Evans
Olivia Jefferson (George's mother): Zara Cully
Florence (the maid): Marla Gibbs
Harry Bentley (a neighbor): Paul Benedict
Helen Willis (a neighbor): Roxie Roker
Tom Willis (Helen's husband): Franklin Cover
Jenny Willis (their daughter): Berlinda Tolbert

Vital Statistics

Half-hour sitcom. CBS.
First aired: Jan. 18, 1975
Most popular time shot: Sunday, 9:30-10:00 PM
Last show: Renewed for 1984-1985 season
Rated in a year's Top 25: 1976 (21), 1977 (24), 1980 (8), 1981 (6) 1982 (4), 1983 (11), 1984 (19)

INSIDE FACTS

HOW ISABEL SANFORD "MOVED ON UP":

- She left her husband in New York, taking her three kids with her to California.
- She got work in a show called *Amen Corner*, which director Stanley Kramer went to see.
- He liked her performance so much that he offered her a part as a cook in the Academy Award-winning *Guess Who's Coming To Dinner.*
- This led to numerous guest appearances on the *Carol Burnett Show.*
- Which led to Norman Lear's calling her to audition for a part in *All In The Family* — as Lionel's aunt.
- The next year, she became Lionel's mother, Louise, and when *The Jeffersons* was spun off into a series she "moved on up" with it.

TRIVIA QUIZ

THE SUBJECT IS ... BLACK ACTORS AND ACTRESSES:

It wasn't until the '60s and '70s that TV moguls included blacks in starring roles. Here are five characters played by blacks. Can you name the actor/actress?
1. Alexander Scott, tennis trainer.
2. Barney Collier, electronics expert.
3. Florida Evans, a maid
4. Lt. Uhura, communications officer
5. Linc Hayes, *Mod Squd* member

ANSWERS:
1. Bill Cosby
2. Greg Morris
3. Esther Rolle
4. Nichelle Nichols
5. Clarence Williams III

Well, we're movin' on up
To the east side.
To a deluxe apartment in the sky.
Movin' on up
To the east side.
We fin'ly got a piece of the pie.

Fish don't fry in the kitchen;
Beans don't burn on the grill
Took a whole lot o' tryin'
Just to get up that hill.
Now we're up in the big leagues
Gettin' our turn at bat.
As long we live,
It's you and me baby,
There ain't nothin wrong with that.

Well, we're movin' on up
To the east side.
To a deluxe apartment in the sky.
Movin' on up
To the east side.
We fin'ly got a piece of the pie.

37

THE SHOW: A classic comedy based on characters created by Charles Addams for his cartoons in *The New Yorker*. Each week, we were invited into the Victorian mansion at 000 Cemetery Lane to visit Gomez Addams and his family: his lovely wife Morticia (who might be feeding her man-eating plant, Cleopatra), daughter Wednesday (carrying Marie Antoinette, her headless doll), and his son Puggsley (with his pet octopus Aristotle). Also on hand: Lurch the butler, who spoke

John Astin, the perfect Gomez Addams.

mostly in groans, Cousin Itt, a four-foot ball of hair, Uncle Fester (so charged with electricity that he could light a light bulb in his mouth), and a variety of other creatures. Perfectly normal, right? Well *they* thought so. Whenever an innocent visitor ran out of the house screaming, Morticia would shake her head and say: "Poor man, his job is getting to him."

THE SONG: Written by the author of the *Green Acres* theme. Don't forget to snap your fingers.

Main Cast

Gomez Addams: John Astin
Morticia Addams (his wife): Carolyn Jones
Wednesday Addams (their daughter): Lisa Loring
Puggsley Addams (their son): Ken Weatherwax
Uncle Fester: Jackie Coogan
Lurch (the butler): Ted Cassidy
Thing (a hand in a box): A hand
Cousin Itt (who knows?): Felix Silla

Vital Statistics

Half-hour sitcom. ABC. 64 episodes.
First aired: Sept. 18, 1964
Time slot: Friday, 8:30 – 9:00 PM (1964-66)
Last show: Sept. 2, 1966
Ranked in a year's Top 25: 1965 (23)

INSIDE FACTS

ABOUT THE STARS:
• John Astin had starred in a previous series, *I'm Dickens, He's Fenster,* in 1962.
• At one time Jackie Coogan, Uncle Fester, was Hollywood's biggest child star. His best-known film: *The Kid.* The Addams Family resurrected him from obscurity.
• Ted Cassidy, a seven-footer, had a hard time getting work as an actor until Lurch.

MISCELLANEOUS:
• Charles Addams hadn't ever named his characters in *The New Yorker* cartoons. He did so specifically for the TV program.
• From 1964-66, the *Addams Family* aired as a Saturday morning cartoon. In this series, they traveled around the country in a camper.

TRIVIA QUIZ

1. What did Gomez call Morticia?
2. What language drove Gomez crazy?
3. Whose uncle was Fester?
4. What was Gomez's profession?
5. Wednesday had a pet named Homer. What kind of creature was it?

38

They're creepy and they're kooky
Mysterious and spooky
They're altogether ooky
THE ADDAMS FAMILY

Their house is a museum
Where people come to see 'em
They really are a scream
THE ADDAMS FAMILY

(da-da-da-dum-snap fingers) Neat
(da-da-da-dum-snap fingers) Sweet
(da-da-da-dum, da-da-da-dum,
 da-da-da-dum-snap fingers) Petite

So get a witches shawl on
A broomstick you can crawl on
We're gonna pay a call on
THE ADDAMS FAMILY

39

I Love Lucy

THE SHOW: Lucy MacGillicuddy married Ricky Ricardo, a Cuban-born bandleader who worked at the Tropicana Club in New York City, and they moved into an apartment owned by Fred and Ethel Mertz (who were also their next-door neighbors and best friends). Ricky just expected Lucy to be a "normal" housewife, but he soon discovered there was nothing "normal" about Lucy. She managed to turn even the simplest domestic chores into disasters (like the time she was pinned to the wall of her kitchen by her runaway loaf of bread). On top of that, Lucy longed to be in show business, and used

Desi sang I Love Lucy on the show.

every trick she could think of to get into Ricky's show . . . which, of course, drove Ricky crazy. Get the picture? It went on for seven years, and America never got tired of it. In fact, it's *still* a re-run favorite!

THE SONG: One of TV's most famous instrumental themes, but these are the original lyrics. Desi sang them on the show (remember?). It was a disco hit in 1977.

Main Cast

Lucy Ricardo: Lucille Ball
Ricky Ricardo (her husband): Desi Arnaz
Fred Mertz (a neighbor): William Frawley
Ethel Mertz (a neighbor): Vivian Vance
Little Ricky (Lucy's son): Richard Keith
Betty Ramsey (a neighbor): Mary Jane Croft
Ralph Ramsey (a neighbor): Frank Nelson

Vital Statistics

Half-hour sitcom. CBS. 179 episodes.
First aired: Oct. 15, 1951
Most popular time slot: Monday, 9 – 9:30 PM (1951-57)
Last show: June 24, 1957
Ranked in a year's Top 25: 1952 (3), 1953 (1), 1954 (1), 1955 (1), 1956 (2), 1957 (1)

INSIDE FACTS

MISCELLANEOUS:
- *I Love Lucy* was the first show ever filmed.
- In 1950, when Lucy was offered a show of her own, she insisted that her husband, Desi, be her TV husband, too.
- CBS rejected the idea, saying that no one in America would believe it.
- So Lucy and Desi toured the country doing live performances to prove the idea worked.
- Finally, CBS gave in, but made the couple produce their own pilot.
- In the pilot, Lucy and Desi played themselves — a Hollywood actress and a famous bandleader.
- The sponsor suggested they scale the show down to a lower-class lifestyle, and *I Love Lucy* was born.

TRIVIA QUIZ

1. *I Love Lucy* had a bigger TV audience than Ike's inauguration on Jan. 19, 1953. What was the attraction?
2. In the 1956-57 season, Ricky Ricardo opened his own night club. What was it called?
3. *Lucy* was the #1 show four of the five years from 1953 to 1957. What was the game show that beat it to the #1 spot in 1956?
4. Was Lucille Ball a natural redhead?
5. When Lucy was pregnant, she wasn't allowed to use that word on TV. What did she have to call her "condition"?
ANSWERS

5. "Expectant"
4. Nope
3. *The $64,000 Question*
2. The Babaloo Club
1. Little Ricky's birth

There's a certain couple that I know.
They're strictly love birds,
A pair of turtle dove birds.
He's a guy who wants the world to know.
So ev-'ry day
You'll hear him say

I LOVE LUCY and she loves me,
We're as happy as two can be,
Sometimes we quarrel but then
How we love making up again.

Lucy kisses like no one can,
She's my missus and I'm her man;
And life is heaven you see
'Cause I LOVE LU-CY,
Yes, I LOVE LU-CY
and Lu-cy loves me.

A Song From A Sponsor

Double Your Pleasure

By Mike Chan and Dick Cunliffe

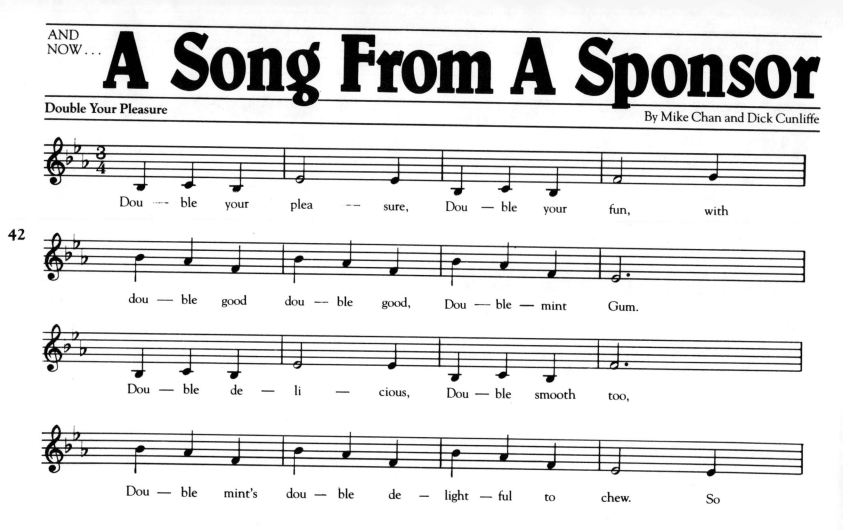

Dou — ble your plea — sure, Dou — ble your fun, with

42

dou — ble good dou — ble good, Dou — ble — mint Gum.

Dou — ble de — li — cious, Dou — ble smooth too,

Dou — ble mint's dou — ble de — light — ful to chew. So

dou — ble your plea — sure, dou — ble your fun,

Get dou — ble ev' — ry — thing rolled in — to one, Oh,

dou — ble your plea — sure, Dou — ble your fun, with

dou — ble good, dou — ble good, Dou — ble — mint Gum.

Happy Days

THE SHOW: From the moment the platter dropped onto the jukebox turntable in the opening credits, to Fonzie's last "Ayyy," you knew that "Happy Days" meant the '50s . . . when girls wore bobby socks, boys wore letter sweaters, and they all hung out down at the malt shop (in this case, Arnold's) after school. *Happy Days* featured the Cunninghams, an All-American sitcom family who lived in Milwaukee: Richie (a "typical" high school student), Howard (a "typical" good-natured white-collar dad), Marion (a "typical" daffy housewife), and Joanie (a "typical" bratty sister). Richie's friends were "typical," too . . . except for The Fonz, a greaser who reigned as the King of Cool. Fonzie became a pop culture hero and for years, millions of American kids imitated his "thumbs up" sign and told their parents to "sit on it."

Henry Winkler, TV's immortal Fonzie.

THE SONG: Original theme: Bill Haley's *Rock Around The Clock*. In 1976, a new theme song was introduced; it hit #5 on the national charts for Pratt and McClain.

Main Cast

The Fonz : Henry Winkler
Richie Cunningham: Ron Howard
Howard Cunningham (his father): Tom Bosley
Marion Cunningham (his mother): Marion Ross
Joanie Cunningham (his sister): Erin Moran
Potsie Weber (Richie's friend): Anson Williams
Ralph Malph (Richie's friend): Donny Most
Chachi Arcola (Fonzie's cousin): Scott Baio
Al Delvecchio (Arnold's owner): Al Molinaro

Vital Statistics

Half-hour sitcom. ABC. 255 episodes.
First aired: Jan. 15, 1974
Most popular time slot: Tuesday, 8 – 8:30 PM
Last show: May 8, 1984
Ranked in a year's Top 25: 1976 (11), 1977 (1), 1978 (2), 1979 (4), 1980 (17), 1981 (15), 1982 (19)

INSIDE FACTS

MISCELLANEOUS:
• Fonzie's leather jacket is now a part of the Smithsonian Institution's permanent collection.
• Fonzie was originally billed seventh in the credits, behind Potsie and Richie's older brother.
• The focus of the show was *going* to be naive Richie's friendship with "worldly" Potsie. But Henry Winkler was so effective that *he* became Richie's (and everyone else's) counterpoint.
• *Happy Days* originated as a story on *Love, American Style*, in Feb. 1972. It was called *Love and the Happy Day*, featuring Ron Howard and Anson Williams.
• Buffalo Bob Smith, of Peanut Gallery and *Howdy Doody* fame, once made an appearance on the show.

TRIVIA QUIZ

1. Which *Happy Days* star co-starred with Henry Fonda in the 1971 TV series, *The Smith Family*?
2. Which star was a regular on *The Debbie Reynolds Show, The Dean Martin Show,* and *The Sandy Duncan Show*?
3. Why was Richie stationed in Greenland (in the army)?
4. In which film before *Happy Days* did Henry Winkler play a greaser?
5. The original Arnold, Pat Morita, quit to star in which TV series?

ANSWERS:
1. Ron Howard.
2. Tom Bosley.
3. Because he'd left the show.
4. *The Lords of Flatbush.*
5. *Mr. T and Tina.*

44

Happy Days

Lyrics: Norman Gimbel, Music: Charles Fox

Sunday, Monday, Happy Days;
Tuesday, Wednesday, Happy Days;
Thursday, Friday, Happy Days;
Saturday,
What a day,
Rockin' all week with you.

Chorus:
This day is ours,
Won't you be mine. (Oh Happy Days)
This day is ours,
Oh please be mine. (Oh Happy Days)

Hello sunshine, goodbye rain,
She's wearin' my high school
　　ring on a chain.
She's my steady, I'm her man,
I'm gonna love her all I can.

CHORUS

45

Gonna cruise her 'round the town,
Show ev'rybody what I've found.
Rock'n'roll with all my friends,
Hopin' the music never ends.

These Happy Days
are yours and mine (Oh Happy Days)
These Happy Days
are yours and mine (Oh Happy Days)
These Happy Days
are yours and mine, Happy Days.

I Married Joan

Joan Davis, before she "married" Judge Bradley Stevens.

THE SHOW: Joan Stevens has done it again! Thinking her husband's new golf clubs will make the perfect gardening tools, she uses them as hoes . . . and breaks every single one! Now he's decided he wants to go golfing! Thinking fast, she locks the door of the closet where he keeps the clubs, and throws the key out the window. "The door is stuck, dear. We'll have to call a carpenter. It shouldn't take him more than a month to fix it." "But I want to go golfing *now*," Judge Stevens moans. Just then, the doorbell rings; it's the mailman. "I was passing by, and this key hit me on the head," he says . . . and Joan's in trouble *again*. For three years Joan Davis found imaginative ways to foul up domestic life for Jim Backus, making this one of the most popular sitcoms on TV. Then in 1955, she retired, saying she was exhausted.

THE SONG: Sung a capella by the Roger Wagner Chorale.

Main Cast

Joan Stevens: Joan Davis
Judge Bradley Stevens (her husband): Jim Backus
Mabel (a friend): Geraldine Carr
Charlie (Mabel's husband): Hal Smith
Beverly Grossman (Joan's sister): Beverly Wills
Janet Tobin (a friend): Sheila Bromley
Kerwin Tobin (Janet's husband): Dan Tobin

Vital Statistics

Half-hour sitcom. NBC. 98 episodes.
First aired: Oct. 15, 1952
Time slot: Wednesday, 8:00 – 8:30 PM (1952-55)
Last show: April 6, 1955
Never ranked in the Top 20 shows of a year.

INSIDE FACTS

ABOUT JOAN DAVIS:
• She started in vaudeville when she was young, touring for five years before she returned home to finish high school.
• Graduating to film, she made six films per year during the '30s.
• She starred in movies like *Hold That Co-ed* (a football/college comedy), with Lionel Barrymore and George Murphy, in 1937.
• She was once voted America's favorite comedienne.
• She was a regular on Rudy Vallee's radio program; in 1943 she got her own — *The Joan Davis Show*, which became *Love That Joan*.
• When she moved to TV, she brought Jim Backus, with whom she'd worked on radio.
• She produced *I Married Joan* herself.

TRIVIA QUIZ

THE SUBJECT IS . . . STARS OF THE '30s

True or false: like Joan Davis, these film stars of the '30s had their own TV series.

1. Jean Arthur.
2. Marlene Dietreich.
3. Judy Garland.
4. Ethel Waters
5. Carole Lombard.

ANSWERS

1. True. *The Jean Arthur Show*, 1966.
2. False.
3. True. *The Judy Garland Show*, 1963-64.
4. True. *Beulah*, 1950-52
5. False.

I Married Joan

Lyrics and Music: Richard Mack

I mar — ried Joan   What a girl, What a whirl, What a life   Oh,

I mar — ried Joan   What a mind,   love is blind, what a   wife

Gid — dy and   gay,   all day she keeps my heart laugh-in' Nev-er know where her brain has flown

Each   to   his   own   Can't de – ny   that's why I   mar-ried Joan

47

The Courtship of Eddie's Father

THE SHOW: Tom Corbett, a widower, was the editor of Tomorrow magazine. He was a pretty nice guy with a lovable, precocious, seven-year-old son named Eddie. Eddie was convinced that his father would be a lot happier if he got married again, so he took it on himself to play matchmaker. As a result, Tom was confronted with a procession of beautiful women and embarrassing situations, all instigated by Eddie. As the show progressed, the "courtship" began to refer less to women, and more to father and son learning to love and trust each other. Always on hand: the confused Japanese housekeeper, Mrs. Livingston, and "mod" photographer, Norman Tinker (in real life, the show's Executive Producer).

Eddie grows up: Brandon Cruz in 1969 and 1984.

THE SONG: Written and performed by Harry Nilsson, a star whose credits include One and Me And My Arrow as a composer, and The Theme From Midnight Cowboy and Without You (a #1 song) as a singer.

Main Cast

Tom Corbett (the father): Bill Bixby
Eddie Corbett (his son): Brandon Cruz
Mrs. Livingston (the housekeeper): Myoshi Umecki
Norman Tinker (Tom's co-worker): James Komack
Tina Rickles (Tom's secretary): Kristina Holland
Joey Kelly (Eddie's classmate): Jodie Foster
Cissy Drummond (Tom's employer): Tippi Hedren

Vital Statistics

Half-hour sitcom. ABC.
First aired: Sept. 17, 1969
Most popular time slot: Wed. 8:00 – 8:30 PM (1969-70, Jan.-June 1972)
Last show: June 14, 1972
Never ranked in the Top 25 shows of a year.

INSIDE FACTS

BACKGROUND INFO:
● Before it was a TV series, The Courtship of Eddie's Father was both a novel and a film. The novel was written by Mark Toby. The movie was released in 1963, and starred Glenn Ford as Tom and Ronny Howard (of Happy Days and Andy Griffith) as Eddie.

ABOUT THE STARS:
● Bill Bixby, a notorious bachelor, liked working with Brandon Cruz so much that he began talking about settling down and having kids.
● James Komack, Tom's friend in the show, was actually one of Bixby's best friends.
● Bixby had starred in My Favorite Martian, and later had the lead roles in The Magician, and The Hulk.

TRIVIA QUIZ

THE SUBJECT IS . . .
SINGLE PARENTS
The Courtship of Eddie's Father featured a single parent. How many of these sitcom single parents can you name?
1. Niece Kelly's "father" in Bachelor Father
2. The father in My Three Sons
3. The mother in One Day At A Time
4. The father in The Rifleman
5. The "father" in Family Affair
ANSWERS:
5. Bill Davis (Brian Keith)
4. Lucas McCain (Chuck Connors)
3. Ann Romano (Bonnie Franklin)
2. Steve Douglas (Fred MacMurray)
1. Bentley Gregg (John Forsythe)

My Best Friend

Lyrics and Music: Harry Nilsson

49

Peo — ple let me tell you bout my best friend, He's a warm heart — ed person who'll love me till the end. ____ Peo — ple let me tell you bout my best friend, One boy cud — dly joy, my up, my down, my pride and joy

Peo — ple let me   tell you bout him he's so much fun Whe— ther ya   talk   man to man or whe— ther we're

talk — ing son to son 'Cause he's my   best   friend   Yes   he's my

best   friend   La da   chi du *(ad lib scat style Al Fine)*

A Song From A Sponsor

Old Spice

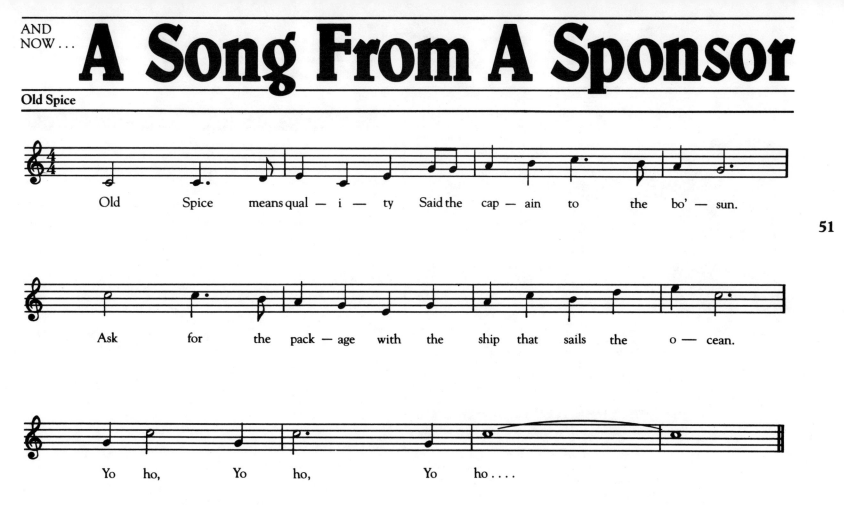

Old Spice means qual — i — ty Said the cap — ain to the bo' — sun.

51

Ask for the pack — age with the ship that sails the o — cean.

Yo ho, Yo ho, Yo ho . . . .

Petticoat Junction

The original cast of Petticoat Junction.

THE SHOW: Kate Bradley was the owner of a secluded hotel near Hooterville called the Shady Rest. Kate didn't have many paying customers (what *did* she do for money?), but she did have her hands full keeping an eye on her three beautiful daughters, and bailing the girls' uncle Joe out of trouble whenever he hatched one of his ridiculous get-rich-quick schemes. Kate was also the only person in town clever enough to outwit Homer Bedlow, vice president of the C. F. & W. Railroad, who was trying to scrap the Hooterville Cannonball, an old steam locomotive that ran between Pixley and Hooterville, and was the local pride and joy.

THE SONG: Sung over the opening credits as the Cannonball rolled down the track, and the Bradley girls skinny-dipped in the water tower, draping their petticoats over the side. Pettico-o-o-at Junction.

Main Cast

Kate Bradley: Bea Benaderet
Uncle Joe Carson: Edgar Buchanan
Billie Jo (a daughter); Jeannine Riley (1963-65), Gunilla Hutton (1965-66), Meredith MacRae (1966-70)
Bobbie Jo (a daughter): Pat Woodell (1963-65), Lori Saunders (1965-70)
Betty Jo (a daughter): Linda Kaye Henning
Homer Bedlow (nasty guy): Charles Lane
Steve Elliot (Betty Jo's husband): Mike Minor

Vital Statistics

Half-hour sitcom. CBS. 148 episodes.
First aired: Sept. 24, 1963
Most popular time slots: Tues. (1964-66), Sat. (1967-70), 9:30-10:00 PM
Last show: Sept. 12, 1970
Ranked in a year's Top 25: 1964 (4), 1965 (15), 1966 (21), 1967 (23).

INSIDE FACTS

ABOUT THE HOOTERVILLE CANNONBALL:
- It was a plastic shell that was originally built for an early Marilyn Monroe film called *Ticket to Tomahawk.*
- It was modeled after a real train in Sonora, California.
- For action shots of the train, the film crew went to Sonora to film.
- There was only one set of wheels for the Cannonball, which were moved from locomotive, to baggage car, to passenger car as scenes required.

ABOUT THE STARS:
- Bea Benaderet had starred in *The George Burns and Gracie Allen Show*, as Blanche.
- She was Lucille Ball's first choice to play Ethel Mertz.
- To pick Kate's daughters, Paul Henning interviewed 1500 women.

TRIVIA QUIZ

1. Which *Petticoat Junction* regular was a wife on *My Three Sons?*
2. Which *Petticoat Junction* cast member was also a regular on *The Lucy Show?*
3. Which *Petticoat Junction* regular was cowboy Hopalong Cassady's sidekick?
4. Which Bradley girl was a regular on *Hee Haw?*
5. Which *Petticoat Junction* regular provided Betty Rubble's voice on *The Flintstones?*

ANSWERS:
1. Meredith MacRae
2. Charles Lane
3. Edgar Buchanan
4. Jeannine Riley, Gunilla Hutton
5. Bea Benaderet

Petticoat Junction

Lyrics: Paul Henning, Music: Curt Massey

Come ride the lit — tle train that is rol — lin' down the tracks at the junc — tion. —

Spoken: Petticoat Junction For — get a — bout your cares, it is time to re —

53

lax at the junc — tion. — *Petticoat Junction* Lot — sa curves, —

you bet, E — ven more — when you

get to the junc — tion, — PET — TI -COAT JUNC - TION.

The Real McCoys

THE SHOW: Well gol-*durn* if *The Real McCoys* ain't the original country sitcom! Back in 1957, the whole McCoy clan moved from West Virginny to a ranch in Californy. An' that cantankerous ol' geezer, Grandpappy Amos, jes' set and rocked on the porch, grousin' about everythin' under the sun and cookin' up schemes to drive everyone plumb loco! His grandson, Luke, was well-meanin' and hard-workin', but sometimes Amos seemed to influence 'im a mite too much fer his own good. That's when Kate, his "sugar babe," stepped in an' straightened 'im out. Kate was a mighty fine gal; she cooked an' cleaned, and did all the things country women 're s'posed to do, includin' takin' care of Luke's sister and brother, Little Luke and "Aunt" Hassie . . . an' she *still* managed to look purty as a picture! Now if she jes' could've gotten ol' Amos to stop complainin' . . . .

THE SONG: A country song, sung sitcom-style. Penned by the author of *I Was An Incubator Baby* (no kidding).

"Grandpappy Amos is delighted to find something to complain about."

Main Cast

Grandpa Amos McCoy: Walter Brennan
Luke McCoy: Richard Crenna
Kate McCoy (his wife): Kathleen Nolan
Aunt Hassie: Lydia Reed
Little Luke: Michael Winkleman
Pepino Garcia (hired hand): Tony Martinez

Vital Statistics

Half-hour sitcom. ABC (1957-62), CBS (1962-63). 224 episodes.
First aired: Oct. 3, 1957
Most popular time slot: Thursday, 8:30-9:00 PM (1957-62)
Last show: Sept. 22, 1963
Ranked in a year's Top 25: 1959 (8), 1960 (11), 1961 (5), 1962 (14)

INSIDE FACTS

ABOUT THE STARS:
• Kathy Nolan played Wendy in the Broadway and TV musical, *Peter Pan* (starring Mary Martin).
• Her real name is Jocelyn Schrum.
• She starred in her own short-lived series in 1964, a spin-off of *McHale's Navy* called *Broadside*.
• Richard Crenna was a former child radio star, with over 6000 radio programs to his credit.
• His first major TV role was on *Our Miss Brooks*, from 1952-55, as Walter Denton, a problem student.
• He starred in several other series (notably *Slattery's People*) and movies like *Wait Until Dark*.
• Walter Brennan, a 3-time Oscar winner, didn't want to star in *The Real McCoys* — he had to be convinced, and repeatedly announced he was quitting because he "couldn't do comedy."

TRIVIA QUIZ

**THE SUBJECT IS . . .
THE OSCARS**
Like Walter Brennan, m ny Oscar-winners had TV shows. Name these five.
1. 1975's Best Supporting Actor co-starred in a sitcom, 1950-58
2. 1952's Best Actress was the Baxters' maid from 1961-66
3. 1948's Best Actress became the wife on *Father Knows Best*
4. 1940's Best Actor, for the *Philadelphia Story*, had his own sitcom, 1971-72
5. The Best Supporting Actor of 1973, he re-created the winning role of a college professor on TV.

ANSWERS

1. George Burns
2. Shirley Booth
3. Jane Wyman
4. Jimmy Stewart
5. John Housman

55

The Real McCoys

Lyrics and Music: Harry Ruby

1. Want you to meet the fam — 'ly that's known as THE REAL Mc — COYS. From
2. Liv- in' like good folks should live, As hap py as kids with toys, Ol'

West Vir — gi– nee they came to stay in sun- ny Cal — i — for- ni — ay. Ol'
Grand – pap py A – mos is head of the clan, He roars like a li- on, But he's gen-tle as a lamb. His

Grand – pap – py A mos and the girls and the boys of the fam- i —ly known as THE REAL Mc- COYS.
grand — son Luke keeps beam- ing with joy, Since he made Miss Kate Miss-us Luke Mc — Coy.

56

3. What a house-keep-er Kate is, She's do-in' what she en-joys. No
4. Shar-ing each oth-ers sor-rows, En-joy-in' each oth-ers joys. Like

gal can beat her when it comes to looks, The same can be said about the way she cooks, For
all oth-er fam 'lies, they quar rel and fuss, But it ain't nev-er se — ri — ous, With

Grand-pap-py A-mos and the girls and the boys of the fam-i-ly known as THE REAL Mc — COYS.

57

Bewitched

THE SHOW: Darrin and Samantha Stevens were an average suburban couple. Darrin commuted to his job at a New York ad agency (Mc-Mann and Tate), while Sam was a happy housewife. Perfectly normal. Except that she was also a witch. With a wiggle of her nose, she could clean up her house or conjure up George Washington. Keeping her promise to Darrin, Sam avoided using witchcraft most of the time — which infuriated her mother, Endora, who couldn't understand her attraction to a mortal, and delighted in harrassing "Durwood" with her *own* magic. Other "witches"

Bewitched's hilarious original stars, Elizabeth Montgomery and Dick York.

were friendlier, including: the bumbling Aunt Clara, Dr. Bombay, Uncle Arthur, and Sam's father, Maurice.

THE SONG: Co-written by Howard Greenfield, Neil Sedaka's partner on tunes like *Calendar Girl.* It was performed as an instrumental on the show, while an animated witch flew around the credits.

Main Cast

Samantha Stevens: Elizabeth Montgomery
Darrin Stevens (her husband): Dick York
Darrin Stevens (1969-72): Dick Sargent
Endora (her mother): Agnes Moorhead
Tabitha Stevens (her daughter): The Murphy twins
Larry Tate (Darrin's boss): David White
Louise Tate (his wife): Irene Vernon, Kasey Rogers
Abner Kravitz (a neighbor): George Tobias
Gladys Kravitz: Alice Pearce, Sandra Gould

Vital Statistics

Half-hour sitcom. ABC. 306 episodes.
First aired: Sept. 17, 1964
Most popular time slots: Thurs., 9 – 9:30 PM (1964-67),
Thurs., 8:30 – 9:00 PM (1967-71)
Last show: July 1, 1972
Ranked in a year's Top 25: 1965 (2), 1966 (7), 1967 (8), 1968 (11), 1969 (12), 1970 (25)

INSIDE FACTS

ABOUT BEWITCHED'S ORIGIN:
• The show was originally conceived by William Dozier, creator and Executive Producer of *Batman,* while he was a V.P. at Screen Gems.
• The role of Sam was first offered to British stage actress Tammy Grimes. She turned it down.
• Coincidentally, Elizabeth Montgomery and her husband-to-be, William Asher, approached Dozier with an idea for a sitcom just as Grimes was rejecting *Bewitched.*
• Dozier suggested they do *Bewitched* instead, with Asher directing it. They agreed, so they could be together.
• When shooting began, Montgomery was 8 months pregnant. Asher had to shoot the first 5 shows without her, adding in her parts later.

TRIVIA QUIZ

1. What was the name of *Bewitched's* spinoff series?
2. Elizabeth Montgomery is what famous actor's daughter?
3. Who played Sam's mod sister Serena?
4. What explanation was made on the show for the new Darrin in 1969?
5. What was the Stevens' son named?

ANSWERS:

1. *Tabitha.*
2. Robert Montgomery.
3. Elizabeth Montgomery.
4. None was given.
5. Adam.

Bewitched, bewitched,
You've got me in your spell.
Bewitched, bewitched,
You know your craft so well.
Before I knew what I was doing,
I looked in your eyes.
That brand of woo you've been brewin'
Took me by surprise.

You witch, you witch,
One thing is for sure.
That stuff you pitch
Just hasn't got a cure.
My heart was under lock and key,
But somehow it got unhitched.
I never thought that I could be had,
But now I'm caught and I'm kinda glad
To be Bewitched.

F Troop

THE SHOW: Welcome to Fort Courage, a U.S. Cavalry outpost in Kansas, where reveille is played at 10:00 AM "because of the time difference." The C.O., Capt. Wilton Parmenter, formerly an orderly in charge of officers' laundry, won his commission by sneezing during a Civil War battle (it sounded like "Charge!") . . . The rest of F Troop upholds the same high standards: the lookout is half-blind; the bugler can't play; and Sgt. O'Rourke (along with Cpl. Agarn) is mainly concerned with selling Indian souvenirs to tourists. With friends like that, who needs enemies? Luckily, there aren't any enemies. The Hekawi Indians can't even remember how to do a war dance. "It's like a rain dance, I think, only drier," explains Chief Wild Eagle in one episode.

Forrest Tucker, F Troop's Sgt. O'Rourke.

THE SONG: Apparently, the lyrics were changed for the show; the first verse is the original lyric, but the second verse was used on the air. They're both great.

Main Cast

Capt. Wilton Parmenter (commander): Ken Berry
Sgt. Morgan O'Rourke (hustler): Forrest Tucker
Cpl. Randolph Agarn (his crony): Larry Storch
Wrangler Jane (cowgirl): Melody Patterson
Chief Wild Eagle (Hekawi chief): Frank DeKova
Crazy Cat (chief's assistant): Don Diamond
Hannibal Dobbs (the bugler): James Hampton

Vital Statistics

Half-hour sitcom. ABC. 65 episodes.
First aired: Sept. 14, 1965
Time slots: Tues. 9 – 9:30 PM (1965-66), Thurs. 8-8:30 PM (1966-67)
Last show: Aug. 31, 1967
Never ranked in a year's Top 25 shows.

INSIDE FACTS

ABOUT O'ROURKE AND AGARN:
• Larry Storch and Forrest Tucker each starred in obscure '50s TV series: Storch hosted a variety program called *The Larry Storch Show* on CBS in 1952-53.
• Tucker played the owner of a charter boat service in a syndicated show called *Crunch and Des* in 1955.
• Each of them starred in a series after *F Troop* which only lasted 13 episodes: Storch was in the *Queen and I* with Billy DeWolfe (1969) and Tucker was in *Dusty's Trail* with Bob Denver (1973).
• In 1975, they were reunited in a live-action Saturday morning sitcom called *The Ghost Busters.* In it, they fought the ghosts of Frankenstein's Monster, Dracula, the Mummy, etc., with the help of their gorilla, Tracy.

TRIVIA QUIZ

1. Which *F Troop* cast member really had been in the U.S. Cavalry (really!)?
2. Which *F Troop* regular was only 16 years old when the show was cast?
3. Which *F Troop* regular finally had a hit show of his own — only to have it cancelled because the network wasn't doing that kind of show anymore?
4. Which *F Troop* regular was a voice on cartoons like *Tennessee Tuxedo, Sabrina the Witch, Koko the Clown?*
5. Which *F Troop* cast member was also a regular on *The Doris Day Show* and *Love, American Style.*

ANSWERS:
1. Forrest Tucker
2. Melody Patterson
3. Ken Berry, *Mayberry R.F.D.*
4. Larry Hampton
5. James Storch

60

Theme From "F" Troop

Lyrics: Irving Taylor, Music: William Lava

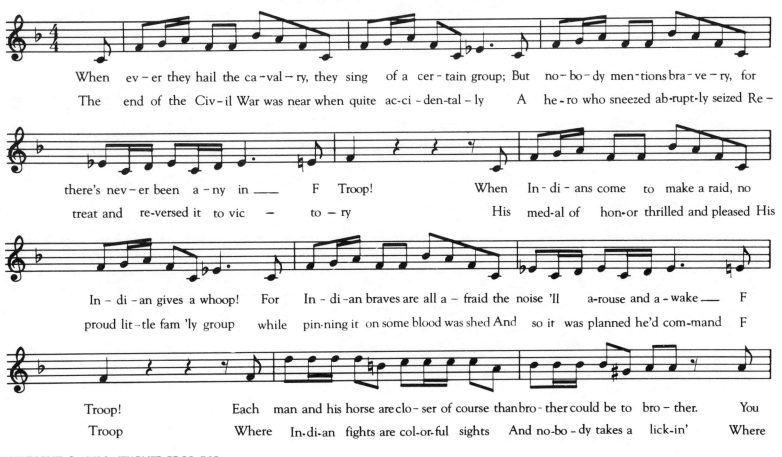

When ev-er they hail the ca-val-ry, they sing of a cer-tain group; But no-bo-dy men-tions bra-ve-ry, for

The end of the Civ-il War was near when quite ac-ci-den-tal-ly A he-ro who sneezed ab-rupt-ly seized Re-

there's nev-er been a-ny in ___ F Troop! When In-di-ans come to make a raid, no

treat and re-versed it to vic — to-ry His med-al of hon-or thrilled and pleased His

In-di-an gives a whoop! For In-di-an braves are all a-fraid the noise 'll a-rouse and a-wake ___ F

proud lit-tle fam'ly group while pin-ning it on some blood was shed And so it was planned he'd com-mand F

Troop! Each man and his horse are clo-ser of course than bro-ther could be to bro-ther. You

Troop Where In-di-an fights are col-or-ful sights And no-bo-dy takes a lick-in' Where

61

just   can't   tell   one   from   the   oth — er.   The   ca – val – ry   al – ways talks of them if
pale — face   and red–skin   Both   turn   chick-en   When kil-ling and   fight•ing get them down They

62

e – ver mo – rale should droop. They   know they can cheer down heart-ed men with tales that are told of the   old — F
know their mo–rale won't droop   As   long as they all re – lax in town   Be

1

2

Troop!!   fore they re sume with a bang and a boom . . .   F   Troop!

Maverick

THE SHOW: *Maverick* started out as a "straight" western about a fancy cowboy who gambled his way around the frontier. Then a bored script-writer decided the star, James Garner, had "beady eyes," and wrote them into a script ("Maverick looks at him with his beady little eyes"). Garner thought it was hilarious, and did the whole scene tongue-in-cheek . . . and the first TV comic western was born. The Maverick Brothers became a special kind of cowboy hero: they couldn't handle guns; they preferred to run rather than fight; and they sought money, not honor. Of course they lent the obligatory help-ing hands to people in trouble. But as likely as not, it was because they thought they could make a buck on it. A Maverick specialty: parodies of other popular westerns, including a *Gunsmoke* lampoon called *Gunshy*, and *Three Queens Full*, about Joe Wheelright at the Subrosa Ranch (*Bonanza*, of course).

James Garner and Jack Kelly, stars of Maverick.

THE SONG: Upbeat, sung by a chorus.

Vital Statistics

Hour-long western. ABC. 124 episodes.
First aired: Sept. 22, 1957
Most popular time slot: Sunday, 7:30 – 8:30 PM (1957-61)
Last show: July 8, 1962
Ranked in a year's Top 25: 1959 (6), 1960 (19)

INSIDE FACTS

HOW BRET'S BROTHER WAS BORN:
● James Garner was originally *Maverick*'s only star.
● But the producers discovered it took more than a week to film each episode, which put them con-stantly behind schedule.
● Their solution: add a "brother," Bart, to alternate with Garner, so they could be shooting two epi-sodes at once.

ABOUT THE STARS:
● Pre-*Maverick*, Garner had been a male model.
● Jack Kelly was a star in the 1956 sci-fi classic, *Forbidden Planet*.
● In 1977, Garner won an Emmy as TV's best dramatic actor, for his role in *The Rockford Files*.
● Kelly's TV experience prior to *Maverick* was primarily as a doctor in soap operas.

TRIVIA QUIZ

1. Maverick replaced TV's most famous amateur variety show. What was it called?
2. Roger Moore went on to play what famous TV detective?
3. Bret and Bart used to quote their "pappy" frequently. Who actually played their father?
4. Jack Kelly starred in three TV series in the '70s. Can you name one?
5. In the 1971-72 season, James Garner returned to TV as a cow-boy. What was the show called?

ANSWERS

1. *The Ted Mack Amateur Hour*
2. Simon Templar, The Saint
3. James Garner
4. *Get Christie Love!*, *The Hardy Boys*, *The NBC Comedy Hour*
5. Nichols

Maverick

Lyrics: Paul Francis Webster, Music: David Buttolph

64

Who is the tall, dark stran—ger there? MAV-ER-ICK is the name!

Rid—in' the trail to who knows where, Luck is his com—pan—ion,

Gam—blin' is his game; Smooth as the han—dle on a gun,

MAV-ER-ICK is the name! Wild as the wind in Or—e—gon,

Blow—in' up a can—yon, Eas—i—er to tame:

Riv—er boat, ring your bell, ___ Fare thee well, An—na—bel! ___

Luck is the la—dy that He loves the best, ___

Natch—ez to New Or—leans, ___ Liv—in' on jacks and queens, ___

MAV—ER—ICK is a leg—end of the West, ___

MAV—ER—ICK is the leg—end of the West. ___

65

The Roy Rogers Show

THE SHOW: As he arrived at his Double R Bar Ranch, outside of Mineral City, it suddenly occurred to Roy Rogers that there was something strange about the old Barnum place. If it really was deserted, then why had he seen a wisp of smoke rising from the chimney? Of course! That's where the rustlers were holed up! Roy jumped on Trigger's back and took off in a flash, with Bullet the Wonder Dog running alongside. His sidekick, Pat Brady, hopped into his jeep (Nellybelle), trying to keep up. The jeep wouldn't start. "C'mon girl," the grizzled cowboy moaned as the vehicle finally turned over; and Pat took off in hot pursuit. Meanwhile, Roy had arrived at the ramshackle ranch house. He circled until he spotted one of the bad guys. Blam! He got 'im! Blam! he got the other one, and had 'em both roped and tied by the time Pat got there. Hooray for the King of the Cowboys!

The King of the Cowboys and the Queen of the Sagebrush.

THE SONG: Written by Dale Evans and sung at the close of every episode by Roy and Dale, in close harmony.

Main Cast

Roy Rogers (good guy): Roy Rogers
Dale Evans (his wife): Dale Evans
Pat Brady (his sidekick): Pat Brady
Ralph Cotton (the mayor): Harry Lauter
The Sons of the Pioneers (Rogers' singing group)

Vital Statistics

Half-hour western. NBC (1951-57), CBS (Sat. morning 1961-64)
101 episodes.
First aired: Dec. 30, 1951
Most popular time slot: Sunday, 6:30 – 7:00 PM (1951-57)
Last show: June 23, 1957
Never ranked in the Top 20 of a year.

INSIDE FACTS

ABOUT THE STARS

• Rogers' real name was Leonard Slye.
• He was originally from Cincinnati.
• Roy Rogers was 39 years old when the show debuted (1951).
• He and Dale were married in 1947 (she had been his leading lady in films).
• Trigger, his horse, was purchased in 1938 for $2500 — a bargain, considering what he was worth to Rogers over the next 20 years.
• Roy performed most of his own stunts on the show.
• Roy and Dale returned to TV in 1962 with a variety program called *The Roy Rogers and Dale Evans Show* — It lasted only three months.

TRIVIA QUIZ

1. What kind of dog was Bullet, the "Wonder Dog"?
2. What was Dale's horse's name?
3. What did Roy do with Trigger after Trigger's death?
4. Roy's chief rival on TV was a singing cowboy with a horse named Champion. Who was he?
5. Another rival on the TV range: William Boyd, also known as _____ .

ANSWERS

1. A German Shepherd.
2. Buttermilk. Very wholesome.
3. He had Trigger stuffed and mounted.
4. Gene Autry.
5. Hopalong Cassidy.

Some trails are happy ones,
Others are blue.
It's the way you ride the trail that counts,
Here's a happy one for you.

Happy trails to you,
Until we meet again.
Happy trails to you,
Keep smilin' until then.

Who cares about the clouds
When we're together?
Just sing a song,
And bring the sunny weather.

67

Happy trails to you,
Till we meet a-gain.

(Repeat, from the first "Happy Trails")

AND
NOW...
A Song From A Sponsor

I'm Chiquita Banana

Written by Len MacKenzie, Garth Montgomery, and William Wirges

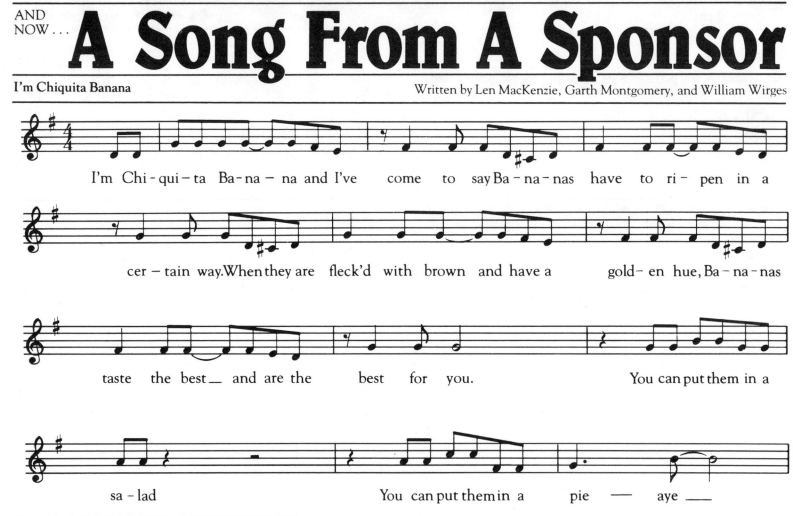

I'm Chi-qui-ta Ba-na—na and I've come to say Ba-na-nas have to ri-pen in a

68

cer—tain way. When they are fleck'd with brown and have a gold-en hue, Ba-na-nas

taste the best __ and are the best for you. You can put them in a

sa-lad You can put them in a pie — aye __

An~ y ~way you want to eat them

It's im—pos—si—ble to

beat them. But ba — na~nas like the cli~mate of the ve~ry, ve~ry tro~pi~cal e —

69

qua - tor. _____ So you should ne-ver put ba — na — nas ____

in the re — fri — ge — ra - tor. No no no no!

Cheyenne

THE SHOW: *Cheyenne* debuted in 1955 as one of three alternating segments on *Warner Brothers Presents.* All

Clint Walker, star of Cheyenne.

three were based on successful movies (*Cheyenne* was a 1947 film starring Dennis Morgan; the other two were *Casablanca* and *King's Row*), but only *Cheyenne* survived the leap to TV. Set in the 1860s, the show featured huge Clint Walker as a lonely cowboy named Cheyenne Bodie — a half-breed (he was half Cheyenne Indian) whose fate seemed to be a life of endless wandering. Bodie was never in the same place two episodes in a row; he might be a wagon train scout one week, then show up as a ranch hand or a deputy sheriff in the next installment. Though he was powerfully built and 6'7" tall, Cheyenne was on the losing end of a lot of fights — a fact which Walker guessed added to the show's popularity. "People like to see a big guy like me get beat up," he said.

THE SONG: Slow, sad, and memorable. Sung by a chorus.

Main Cast

Cheyenne Bodie (drifting cowboy): Clint Walker
Smitty (his companion): L. Q. Jones

Vital Statistics

Hour-long western. ABC. 107 episodes.
First aired: Sept. 20, 1955
Time slots: Tues., 7:30 – 8:30 PM (1955-59),
Mon., 7:30 – 8:30 PM (1959-62)
Last show: Sept. 13, 1963
Ranked in a year's Top 25: 1958 (13), 1959 (18), 1960 (17)

INSIDE FACTS

THE CONTROVERSY:

● In 1958, *Cheyenne* was in the Top 20, and Clint Walker was an up-and-coming star.
● He asked Warner Brothers to re-negotiate his contract; he wanted them to waive their right to 50% of all his personal appearance fees, and asked for a percentage of the show's profits (as other stars had).
● Warner Brothers refused outright, so Walker walked out of the show.
● Warner's replaced him with Ty Hardin (as Bronco Layne), still calling the show *Cheyenne* (*Bronco* later became a series on its own.)
● Walker finally returned, but was still unhappy. He felt the role was used up — but with *Cheyenne* still in the Top 20, Warner's kept it going until 1963.

TRIVIA QUIZ

THE SUBJECT IS . . . LONERS
Cheyenne Bodie was a classic cowboy loner. Here are some other TV loners; see if you can name the shows they appeared on.
1. Dr. Richard Kimble (David Janssen)
2. Jason McCord (Chuck Connors)
3. Josh Randall (Steve McQueen)
4. Paul Bryan (Ben Gazzara)
5. John Reid (Clayton Moore)

ANSWERS:

1. *The Fugitive*
2. *Branded*
3. *Wanted: Dead or Alive*
4. *Run For Your Life*
5. *The Lone Ranger*

Cheyenne

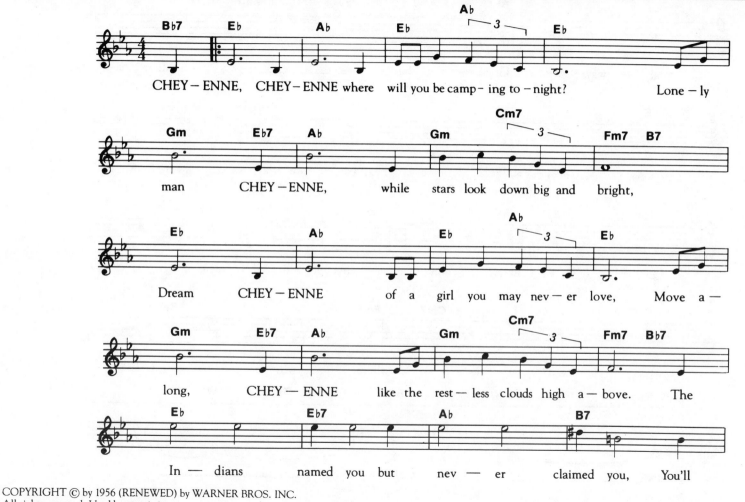

CHEY – ENNE, CHEY – ENNE where will you be camp – ing to – night? Lone – ly

man CHEY – ENNE, while stars look down big and bright,

Dream CHEY – ENNE of a girl you may nev – er love, Move a –

long, CHEY – ENNE like the rest – less clouds high a – bove. The

In – dians named you but nev – er claimed you, You'll

71

al — ways be lone — ly but free, _____ Move a —

long, CHEY — ENNE the next pas — ture's al — ways so green, Drift — in'

on, CHEY — ENNE don't for- get what you've al- read- y seen, And

when you set — tle down where will it be CHEY —

ENNE. _____ CHEY — ENNE. _____

72

The Life and Legend of Wyatt Earp

THE SHOW: Hugh O'Brian played Wyatt Earp in TV's first "adult" western. Clad head-to-toe in black, with his two oversized Buntline Specials tucked into their holsters, U.S. Marshall Earp patrolled the streets of Ellsworth, Dodge City, and Tombstone during the show's six-year run. What made it unique was historical accuracy and character development, unheard of in TV sagebrush dramas until then. E.g., the last episodes covered Earp's most famous moment, the Gunfight at the OK Corral, when he broke the power of the Clanton Gang.

Hugh O'Brian, star of Wyatt Earp.

THE SONG: This was the only TV theme composed by one of Hollywood's most honored songwriters, Harry Warren. Warren wrote *Jeepers Creepers, We're In The Money, I Only Have Eyes For You, You Must Have Been a Beautiful Baby, That's Amore,* and many more. The lyrics were penned by Harold Adamson who also wrote *I Love Lucy*'s lyrics.

Main Cast

Wyatt Earp: Hugh O'Brian
Shotgun Gibbs (his deputy): Morgan Woodward
Doc Holliday (his friend): Douglas Fowley
John Behan (his enemy): Steve Brodie
Bat Masterson (his friend): Mason Dinehart III
Doc Goodfellow (his friend): Damian O'Flynn
Old Man Clanton (his enemy): Trevor Bardette
Hal Norton (a deputy): William Tannen

Vital Statistics

Half-hour western. ABC. 266 episodes.
First aired: Sept. 6, 1955
Time slot: Tuesday, 8:30 – 9:00 PM (1955-61)
Last show: Sept. 26, 1961
Ranked in a year's Top 25: 1957 (19), 1958 (6), 1959 (10), 1960 (20)

INSIDE FACTS

MISCELLANEOUS:
● Hugh O'Brian studied Wyatt Earp's life for months before the series started, using a book called *Wyatt Earp* as his guide.
● *Wyatt Earp* was written by Arthur Lake, who had lived with Earp in the last four years of his life. Lake served as "technical adviser" to the show.
● O'Brian was the same size as Earp, 6', 180 pounds.
● O'Brian believed in Wyatt Earp, telling *TV Guide* "I'm convinced that Earp was a thoroughly honest man, righteous, utterly fearless."
● O'Brian was the first of several cowboy stars to demand renegotiating his contract, asking for a 5% ownership in the show. Eventually, he got it.

TRIVIA QUIZ

REAL HEROES:
Like Earp, these real heroes were TV heroes too. Name them.
1. A knife was named after him.
2. Clu Gulager played William Bonney, known as _____ .
3. An ambitious Union general who tried to make a name for himself as an Indian fighter.
4. A cowboy "Robin Hood."
5. A famous Kentucky frontiersman.

ANSWERS
1. Jim Bowie. (*The Adventures of Jim Bowie* — 1956-58)
2. Billy the Kid. (*The Tall Man* — 1960-62)
3. George Custer. (*Custer* — 1967)
4. Jesse James. (*The Legend of Jesse James* — 1965-66)
5. Daniel Boone. (*Daniel Boone* — 1964-70)

The Legend of Wyatt Earp

Lyrics: Harold Adamson, Music: Harry Warren

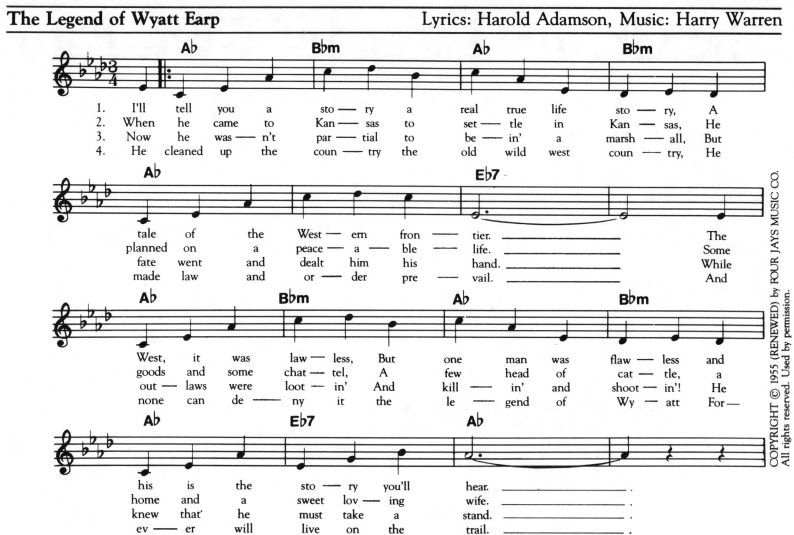

1. I'll tell you a sto — ry a real true life sto — ry, A
2. When he came to Kan — sas to set — tle in Kan — sas, He
3. Now he was — n't par — tial to be — in' a marsh — all, But
4. He cleaned up the coun — try the old wild west coun — try, He

tale of the West — ern fron — tier. _____ The
planned on a peace — a — ble _____ life. _____ Some
fate went and dealt him his _____ hand. _____ While
made law and or — der pre — vail. _____ And

West, it was law — less, But one man was flaw — less and
goods and some chat — tel, A few head of cat — tle, a
out — laws were loot — in' And kill — in' and shoot — in'! He
none can de — ny it the le — gend of Wy — att For —

his is the sto — ry you'll hear. _____ .
home and a sweet lov — ing wife. _____ .
knew that he must take a stand. _____ .
ev — er will live on the trail. _____ .

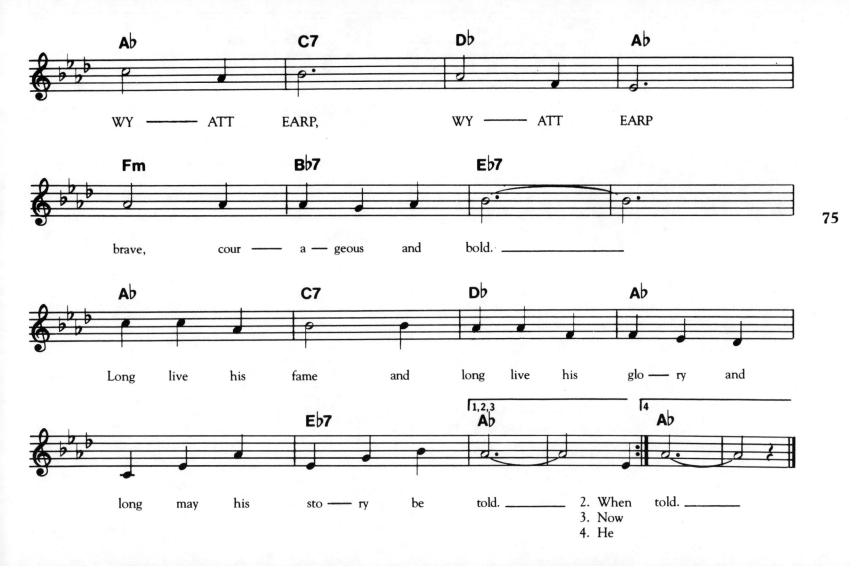

WYATT EARP, WYATT EARP

brave, courageous and bold.

Long live his fame and long live his glory and

long may his story be told. 2. When told.
3. Now
4. He

75

Wagon Train

THE SHOW: *Wagon Train* was a popular western that *didn't* rely on outlaws and gunfights for its stories. Instead: each week, as the caravan headed west, a tale unfolded about one of its members or a guest star who happened to wander in off the Plains (usually the episode was named after the character — "The (*name*) Story"). The wagonmaster for the first four years of the Missouri-to-California trek was grizzled film veteran Ward Bond (Major Seth Adams), a no-nonsense boss who kept a paternal eye on his flock. When Bond died in 1961, John McIntire took the reins as Chris Hale, and guided *Wagon Train* to the #1 spot in TV.

Chris Hale keeps the wagons rollin'.

THE SONG: Performed as an instrumental on the show; it was co-written by two-time Oscar winner Sammy Fain, whose credits include *April Love* and *Love Is A Many Splendored Thing*.

Main Cast

Seth Adams (wagonmaster): Ward Bond
Chris Hale (wagonmaster): John McIntire
Flint McCullough (scout): Robert Horton
Charlie Wooster (cook): Frank McGrath
Bill Hawks (scout): Terry Wilson
Cooper Smith (scout): Robert Fuller

Vital Statistics

Hour, 1½ hour-long western. NBC. 440 episodes.
First aired: Sept. 18, 1957
Most popular time slot: Wednesday, 7:30 – 8:30 PM (1957-62)
Last show: Sept. 5, 1965
Ranked in a year's Top 25: 1958 (23), 1959 (2), 1960 (2), 1961 (2), 1962 (1), 1963 (25)

INSIDE FACTS

MISCELLANEOUS:

• *Wagon Train* was based on the 1950 movie *Wagonmaster*, which starred Ward Bond.
• When he started filming *Wagon Train*, Bond was already a veteran of over 200 cowboy movies.
• *Wagon Train* dueled *Gunsmoke* in the ratings from 1958-1962. Matt Dillon held the *Train* to the #2 position until 1961. Then *Wagon Train* broke through to #1, with *Bonanza* #2, and *Gunsmoke* #3.
• In 1963, *Wagon Train* joined *The Virginian* in attempting a 90-minute format. The experiment only lasted one year.
• John McIntyre, who took over when Ward Bond died in 1961, had been seen as Lt. Dan Muldoon on *Naked City* from 1958-59.

TRIVIA QUIZ

**THE SUBJECT IS...
WESTERNS**
Wagon Train was one of the most popular westerns in TV history. Here are five more. Can you identify them?
1. The star of this show made his screen debut in the title role of the film, *The Thing*.
2. His card read: "Wire Paladin. San Francisco."
3. Chuck Connors played Lucas McCain in _____
4. Steve McQueen played a bounty hunter in _____
5. Barbara Stanwyck was the matriarch of the Barkley family in _____.

ANSWERS:
1. *Gunsmoke*
2. *Have Gun, Will Travel*
3. *The Rifleman*
4. *Wanted: Dead or Alive*
5. *The Big Valley*

(Roll Along) Wagon Train

Lyrics: Jack Brooks, Music: Sammy Fain

77

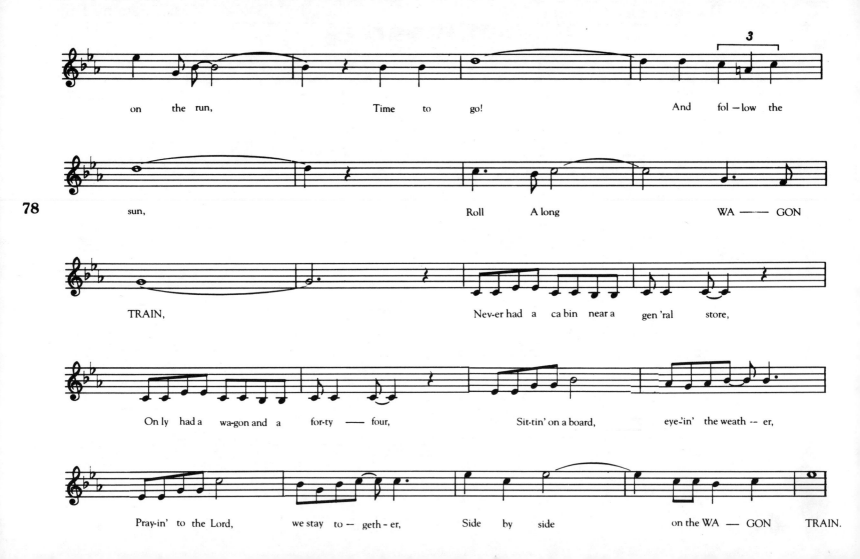

on the run,   Time to go!   And fol—low the

sun,   Roll   A long   WA —— GON

78

TRAIN,   Nev-er had a ca bin near a gen 'ral store,

On ly had a wa-gon and a for-ty —— four,   Sit-tin' on a board,   eye-'in' the weath -- er,

Pray-in' to the Lord,   we stay to — geth-er,   Side by side   on the WA — GON   TRAIN.

Bonanza

THE SHOW: *Bonanza*, the second-most popular western in TV history (*Gunsmoke* is #1), was the saga of Ben "Pa" Cartwright and his three sons: Adam, Hoss, and Little Joe, who ruled a 3000 square mile ranch called The Ponderosa in the 1860s. They were a close-knit family of enormous wealth and power; but they were also likable and down-to-earth: honest, kind, loyal, etc....which helped make them America's most popular Sunday evening house-guests for 11 years.

Two of America's favorite cowboys, Ben and Hoss Cartwright.

THE SONG: Written by "the last of the great songwriters of Hollywood," Jay Livingston and Ray Evans (who also wrote *Mr. Ed*). Among their other classics: *Dear Heart, Tammy, Que Sera, Sera, Mona Lisa,* and *Buttons and Bows.* Performed on the show as an instrumental, the lyrics were sung on TV only once — on *Bonanza*'s premiere. The singers (believe it or not): the Cartwrights, in a segment that's so amusing it's been shown on TV blooper shows! As an instrumental, the song hit #19 for Al Caiola in 1961.

Main Cast

Ben Cartwright (the father): Lorne Greene
Adam Cartwright (#1 son): Pernell Roberts
Hoss Cartwright (#2 son): Dan Blocker
Little Joe Cartwright (#3 son): Michael Landon
Hop Sing (the houseboy): Victor Sen Yung
Roy Coffee (the sheriff): Ray Teal
Candy Canaday (the foreman): David Canary

Vital Statistics

Hour-long western. NBC. 440 episodes.
First aired: Sept. 12, 1959
Most popular time slot: Sunday, 9 – 10:00 PM (1961-72)
Last show: Jan. 16, 1973
Ranked in a year's Top 25: 1962 (17), 1963 (4), 1964 (2), 1965 (1), 1966 (1), 1967 (1), 1968 (7), 1969 (3), 1970 (3), 1971 (9), 1972 (20).

INSIDE FACTS

ABOUT THE STARS:
• NBC wanted established stars for *Bonanza* but the show's creator, David Dortort, insisted that TV could make its own stars.
• Of the four leading men, all but Michael Landon were virtual unknowns.
• Pernell Roberts was a New York stage actor.
• Lorne Greene, who had once been the Canadian Broadcasting Company's main announcer, was selected after Dortort saw him on a *Wagon Train* episode.
• Dan Blocker, a former Texas school teacher, had worked once with Dortort on an episode of *The Restless Gun* (a TV western series).
• Landon had appeared as a guest in many shows, but had never been offered a starring role. "I fixed that," said Dortort.

TRIVIA QUIZ

1. How many times was Ben married?
2. In what 1957 film did Michael Landon star?
3. What was Hoss's "real" first name?
4. How did each episode of *Bonanza* begin?
5. How did the Ponderosa get its name?

ANSWERS

1. Three. Each wife gave him a son.
2. *I Was a Teenage Werewolf.*
3. Eric. Hoss meant "good luck" in Norwegian.
4. A map of the area caught fire.
5. From the abundance of pines on the land.

Bonanza

Lyrics and Music: Jay Livingston and Ray Evans

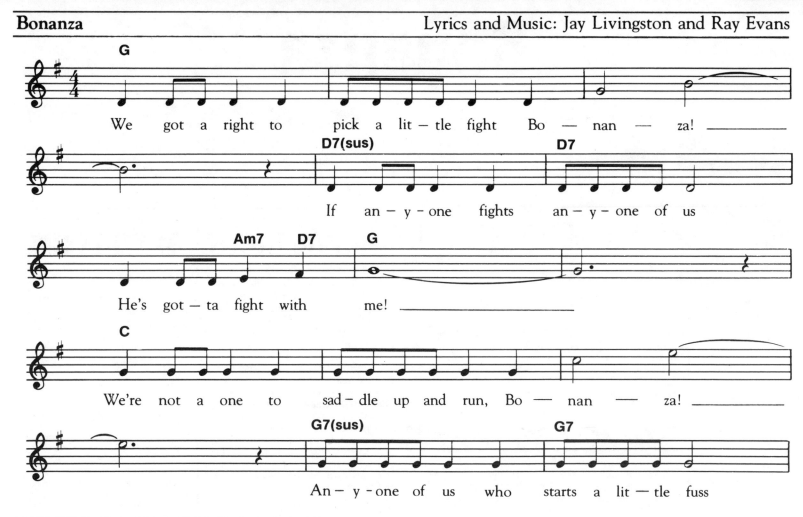

80

We got a right to pick a lit-tle fight Bo — nan — za! _____

If an — y-one fights an — y-one of us

He's got — ta fight with me! _____

We're not a one to sad — dle up and run, Bo — nan — za! _____

An — y-one of us who starts a lit — tle fuss

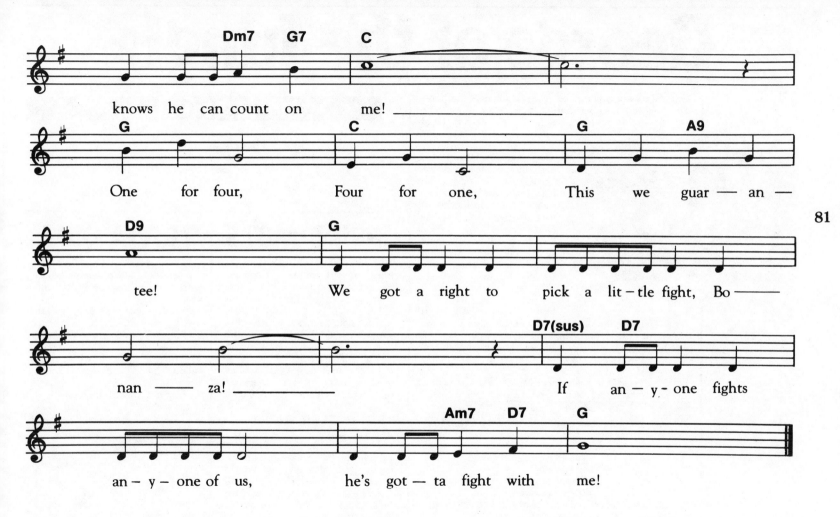

THE SHOW: Sometimes swinging through the jungle was a whole lot harder than "saving the day" for George of the Jungle. Because he always — ALWAYS — smashed into a tree. George was a lovable, bumbling Tarzan-like hero who lived in the Imgwee Gwee Valley in Africa. His mission was to save people in distress, and considering his overall ineptitude, he did pretty well. Always on hand: Ursula, his articulate mate, Ape, his primate companion, Shep, the elephant who thought he was a dog, and Fella, a voluptuous native woman. SUPER CHICKEN: Henry Cabot Henhouse III was a scientist who discovered Super Sauce, a liquid that turned him into a crime fighter with super powers whenever he drank it. On hand to assist him: Fred, his loyal, dimwitted lion companion, who "knew the job was dangerous when he took it."

THE SONGS: One is written by Jay Ward, creator of these characters and many others. Don't forget to cluck.

Two of Jay Ward's cult heroes, George of the Jungle and Super Chicken.

82

Main Cast

George (King of the Jungle)
Ursula (his friend)
Ape (a gorilla)
Shep (an elephant)
Seymour (a plant)
Wiggy (a rhino)
SuperChicken: Henry Cabot Henhouse III
Fred (SuperChicken's pal)

Vital Statistics

Half-hour cartoon show. ABC.
First aired: Sept. 9, 1967
Time slot: Saturday morning
Last show: Sept. 6, 1970

INSIDE FACTS

ABOUT JAY WARD:
• He created the first cartoon series ever made especially for TV: *Crusader Rabbit*, which debuted in 1949.
• His next series, which first appeared in 1959, was a TV classic: *Rocky and His Friends* (later known as *The Bullwinkle Show*).
• In the mid-'60s, Quaker Oats selected him to create a character to go with their new cereal, *Cap'n Crunch*.

THE DUDLEY DORIGHT EMPORIUM:
• Believe it or not, there's a store called the Dudley DoRight Emporium right next to Jay Ward's Studio in Hollywood. It's the mail order headquarters for *George of the Jungle* and *Super Chicken* items. Write to them at: 8200 Sunset Blvd., Hollywood, CA 90046.

TRIVIA QUIZ

Jay Ward's characters are Classics with cult followings. Can you identify these five?
1. Dudley loves Nell, but Nell's in love with _____ .
2. He invented the Wayback machine.
3. The race car driver whose car is called the Thunderbolt Grease Slapper.
4. Cap'n Crunch's nemesis is a pirate named _____ .
5. The moonmen on *Rocky and His Friends* were named _____ .

ANSWERS:

1. Dudley's horse
2. Mr. Peabody
3. Tom Slick
4. Jean LaFoot
5. Gidney and Cloyd

George of the Jungle

Lyrics: Sheldon Allman & Stan Worth, Music: Jay Ward

George, George,
George of the Jungle,
Strong as he can be.
George, George,
George of the Jungle,
Lives a life that's free.

When he gets in a scrape,
He makes his escape
With the help of his friend,
an ape named Ape.
Then away he'll schlep
on his elephant Shep
While Fella and Ursula
Stay in step.

George, George
George of the Jungle,
Friend to you and me.

Watch out for that tree!

83

Super Chicken

Lyrics: Sheldon Allman, Music: Stan Worth

When you find yourself in danger
(cluck, cluck, cluck);
When you're threatened
by a stranger;
When it looks like you will
take a lickin'
There is someone who
Will hurry up and rescue you
Just callllll for Superchicken.

Then if you're afraid, you'll have
to overlook it.
Besides, you knew the job
was dangerous
when you took it (cackle)

He will take his supersauce
And throw the bad guys
for a loss,
And he will bring them in
alive and kickin'
(cluck, cluck, cluck)
There is one thing
you should learn
There's never someone else to turn to,
Callllll for Superchicken (cackle)
Callllll for Superchicken
(cluck, cluck, cluck)

Popeye the Sailor

THE SHOW: Popeye was already a popular comic strip character in the early '30s, when the Fleischer Brothers introduced him in one of their Betty Boop cartoons. So it was no surprise that he was an instant hit at the movies, too. Two months later he had his own cartoon (called "I Yam What I Yam") and for the next twenty years he was one of America's biggest box office attractions. Then in the mid-'50s, the Fleischer cartoons were sold to United Artists for TV syndication and he became a TV star as well. *Popeye* appeared on independent stations all over the country. He was so well received that in 1958 production was begun on 200 new cartoons, to be shown exclusively on TV. "Well blow me down!"

THE SONG: Kids made up their own lyrics (". . . I live in a garbage can . . .") and even Popeye changed the words at the end of some of his cartoons.

Popeye, America's favorite sailor.

84

Main Cast

Popeye the Sailor

Olive Oyl (his girlfriend)
Swee'pea (Olive's nephew)
Bluto (the bad guy)
Wimpy (Popeye's friend)

Vital Statistics

Half-hour cartoon show. Syndicated. 450 cartoons.
First aired: Mid-'50s
Time slots: Determined locally
Last show: Still in syndication

INSIDE FACTS

MISCELLANEOUS:

• Jack Mercer was Popeye's voice for most of the cartoons, and Mae Questel was Olive's. But when Mercer went into the army in the '40s, Questel did BOTH voices!

• Much of the dialogue between Popeye and Olive was ad-libbed in the Fleischer cartoons.

• Ever notice that in some cartoons the bully is Bluto, and in others it's Brutus? The reason: Fleischer called him Bluto, but the '50s cartoons used his original comic strip name, Brutus.

• Popeye's first words were in response to the question (by Olive's brother Castor): "Hey are you a sailor?" He replied: "Ja think I was a cowboy?"

• Popeye won an Academy Award in 1936 for *Sinbad the Sailor*.

TRIVIA QUIZ

Popeye wasn't the only sailor man on TV. These actors were, too. Can you name the sailors they played in regular series?
1. Ernest Borgnine
2. John Astin
3. Dean Jones
4. Richard Basehart
5. Joe Flynn

ANSWERS

1. Lt. Cmdr. Quintin McHale on *McHale's Navy*
2. Lt. Cmdr. Mathew Sherman on *Operation Petticoat*
3. Ensign O'Toole, on the show of the same name
4. Admiral Harriman Nelson, on *Voyage to the Bottom of the Sea*
5. Capt. Wallace Binghamton on *McHale's Navy*

"I'm Popeye the Sailor Man"

Lyrics and Music: Sammy Lerner

I'm Popeye the Sailor Man,
I'm Popeye the Sailor Man.
I'm strong to the "finich"
'Cause I eats me spinach.
I'm Popeye the Sailor Man.

I'm one tough Gazookus
Which hates all Palookas
Wot ain't on the up and square.
I biffs 'em and buffs 'em
And always outroughs 'em
An' none of 'em gets nowhere.

If anyone dasses
to risk my "Fisk",
It's "Boff" an' it's "Wham" un'erstan'?
So keep "Good Be-hav-or"
That's your one life-sav-er
With Popeye the Sailor Man.

85

I'm Popeye the Sailor Man,
I'm Popeye the Sailor Man.
I'm strong to the "finich"
'Cause I eats me spinach.
I'm Popeye the Sailor Man.

Casper the Friendly Ghost

THE SHOW: Casper was a mixed-up little ghost with a personality problem. Instead of *scaring* people, he wanted to be *friends.* A typical Casper cartoon began with him moping around the Enchanted Forest, wishing he had someone to play with. Suddenly he'd spot a bird or a squirrel. "Hi. My name is Casper," he'd say. "Do you want to play with me?" The creature's eyes would bug out of its head as it screamed "A G-G-G-Ghost!!" And it took off like a rocket. By the end of every cartoon, though, Casper had saved the animals, and they sang and danced through the forest. It was corny, but it worked. Casper was as successful on TV as he was in theaters in the late '40s. And he was a mainstay of ABC's Saturday morning programming through most of the '60s.

"The friendliest ghost you've seen."

THE SONG: Written by the composers of Oscar nominee, *Bibbity Bobbity Boo* (from *Cinderella*) and sung cheerily by a chorus. (See *77 Sunset Strip.*)

Main Cast

Casper the Friendly Ghost
Nightmare (the Galloping Ghost)
Wendy (The Good Little Witch)
Spooky (The Tuff Little Ghost)
Pearl (his "goilfriend")
The Ghostly Trio (Casper's scary friends)

Vital Statistics

Half-hour cartoon show. Syndicated/ABC.
First aired: 1953 (syndicated); Oct. 5, 1963 (ABC — *The New Casper Cartoon Show*)
Time slots: Determined locally (syndicated); Sat. morning (ABC)
Last show: Dec. 27, 1969 (ABC)

INSIDE FACTS

ABOUT CASPER'S ORIGIN:
● He was created by Joe Oriolo, the animator who did the 1960s *Felix the Cat* series.
● He first appeared in a 1945 Paramount cartoon called *The Friendly Ghost* (he was nameless).
● He didn't appear again until 1948, and still no one at Paramount considered him a long-lasting character.
● Finally, after a third cartoon in 1949, Paramount decided to give him a name and make a series out of him.
● He was an immediate success, responsible for selling a considerable amount of "Casper" merchandise, and becoming a popular comic book. His later cartoons included characters from the comic books.

TRIVIA QUIZ

THE SUBJECT IS . . . GHOSTS & WITCHES
1. What was the name of the teenage TV witch who originally came from Archie Comics?
2. What was the Ghostly Trio's favorite pastime?
3. What did Spooky wear?
4. Hope Lange starred in the live-action program, *The Ghost and* _____.
5. What color was Wendy's cloak?

ANSWERS:
1. Sabrina
2. Going on "scare raids"
3. A derby hat (a "dolby")
4. Mrs. Muir
5. Red

Casper the Friendly Ghost

Lyrics: Mack David, Music: Jerry Livingston

Casper, the Friendly Ghost,
The friendliest ghost you know.
Though grown-ups might
Look at him with fright,
The children all love him so.

Casper, the friendly ghost,
He couldn't be bad or mean.
He'll romp and play,
Sing and dance all day,
The friendliest ghost you've seen.

He always says hello (hello),
And he's really glad to meetcha.
Wherever he may go,
He's kind to every living creature.

87

Grown-ups don't understand
Why children love him the most.
But kids all know
That he loves them so,
Casper the Friendly Ghost.

AND
NOW...
A Song From A Sponsor

The Oscar Mayer Wiener Song

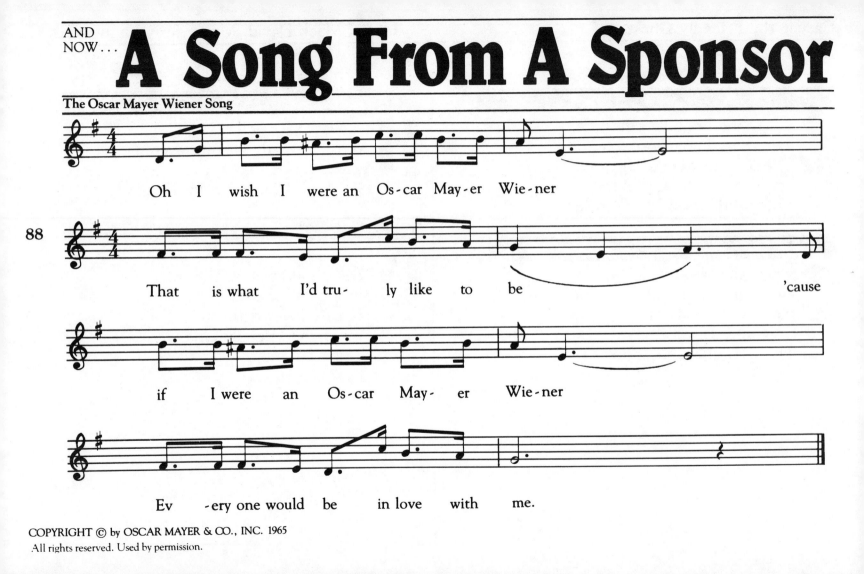

Oh I wish I were an Os-car May-er Wie-ner

88

That is what I'd tru-ly like to be 'cause

if I were an Os-car May-er Wie-ner

Ev -ery one would be in love with me.

A Song From A Sponsor

Choo-Choo Charlie

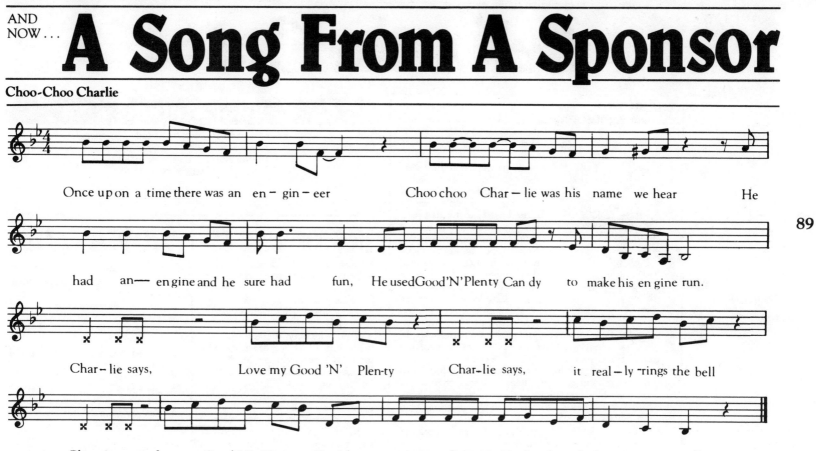

Once up on a time there was an en — gin — eer Choo choo Char — lie was his name we hear He

had an — engine and he sure had fun, He used Good 'N' Plenty Can dy to make his en gine run.

Char — lie says, Love my Good 'N' Plen-ty Char-lie says, it real — ly rings the bell

Char-lie says, Love my Good 'N' Plen-ty Don't know an — y oth-er can-dy that I love so well

Felix the Cat

THE SHOW: Is a black cat bad luck? Not if it's Felix, the most popular cat in cartoon history. Kids watching the syndicated Felix cartoons in the 1960s had no idea he'd been around since 1919, when he appeared in a cartoon called *Feline Follies*. The public loved him, and as Pat Sullivan's studio turned out 26 cartoons a year, his popularity mushroomed. In 1922, he appeared as the New York Yankees' lucky mascot. In 1923, he shared the screen with Charlie Chaplin. In 1927 a Felix doll was Charles Lindbergh's companion as Lindbergh soloed across the Atlantic. Unfortunately, Felix's owner (Sullivan) wasn't interested in "talkies", so silent star Felix was eclipsed by new talking cartoons. His popularity continued in comic strips, but it wasn't until 1960 that he returned in animated form with a new format and a Magic Bag of Tricks that would provide just about anything. In these cartoons, he deftly eluded his arch-enemy, the Professor, who was intent on stealing Felix's Magic Bag.

THE SONG: A light, happy tune sung by a woman at the start and close of each cartoon.

Felix, America's favorite feline.

Main Cast

Felix and his bag of tricks.
Poindexter (Felix's genius friend)
The Professor (Felix's arch-enemy)
Rock Bottom (The Professor's henchman)

Vital Statistics

Half-hour cartoon show. Syndicated. 260 episodes.
First aired: 1960
Time slots: determined locally
Last show: still in syndication

INSIDE FACTS

MISCELLANEOUS

● Felix's was the first image ever to appear on TV. In 1928, when the first experimental TV broadcast occurred, the subject was a Felix doll.

● Otto Messmer, Felix's creator, made him black for practical reasons. "It saves making a lot of outlines, and solid black moves better," he explained.

● The origin of Felix's name: it came from the word "felicity", which means "great happiness".

● In the early cartoons, Felix's secret weapon was his tail, not a bag of tricks. He was able to remove the tail and use it as a hook or a bridge, etc.

● Joe Oriolo, animator of the '60s' *Felix* series, also created *Casper the Friendly Ghost* in 1945.

TRIVIA QUIZ

THE SUBJECT IS ...CATS

Felix was one of the many cartoon cats popular on TV. See if you can name the following cats:
1. His main goal in life was to make a little yellow bird his dinner.
2. A red-nosed cat who appeared on Casper's show with a mouse named Herman.
3. He led a band of street cats on his own prime time show.
4. An Academy Award winner whose partner was Jerry Mouse.
5. Pixie and Dixie tormented him on *Huckleberry Hound*.

ANSWERS
1. Sylvester Cat
2. Katnip
3. Top Cat
4. Tom Cat
5. Jinks the Cat

Felix the Cat

Lyrics: Alfred Bryan   Music: Pete Wendling and Max Kortlander

Fe —— lix the Cat, the won-der-ful, won-der-ful cat, When ev — er he gets in a fix, he

reach- es in – to his bag of tricks Fe —— lix the Cat, the won-der-ful, won-der-ful cat, You'll

laugh so much your sides will split, Your heart will go pit-ter pat watch-ing Fe – lix the Won-der-ful Cat

COPYRIGHT © 1955 by FISHER MUSIC Corp.
1 Times Square Plaza, New York, NY 10036

The Mighty Mouse Playhouse

THE SHOW: Saturday morning: a bunch of kids are sitting in front of the TV, eating their cold cereal. On-screen, Mighty Mouse is relaxing on an asteroid in outer space. Suddenly he hears a cry. It's Pearl Pureheart, back on earth, trying to fight off Oil Can Harry (a cat dressed in a zoot suit), as he grabs her and carries her to his 1940s car. "Is there no one who can save her?" cries the announcer. It's the moment the kids have been waiting for. Our Hero leaps to his feet, singing "Here I come to save the day," and dives headlong to earth. Oil Can Harry tries to make a getaway, but he's no match for you-know-who. Wham! And Pearl is safe again. This went on for twelve years, making Mighty Mouse Playhouse one of Saturday morning's longest-running cartoon shows.

THE SONG: Sung opera-style, because most M.M. cartoons were mini-operas, with cats and mice singing their way through the action.

"Here I come to save the day!"

Main Cast

Mighty Mouse (superhero)
Pearl Pureheart (his girlfriend)
Oil Can Harry (the bad guy; a cat)
Narrator: Tom Morrison (also M.M.'s voice)
Other cartoons featured:
Heckle and Jeckle (talking magpies),
Gandy Goose, Dinky Duck, and others.

Vital Statistics

Half-hour cartoon show. CBS. 150 episodes.
First aired: Dec. 10, 1955
Time slot: Saturday morning
Last show: Sept. 2, 1967

INSIDE FACTS

ABOUT MIGHT MOUSE:
• He was the most popular character in Paul Terry's *Terrytoon* cartoon series.
• He was inspired by Superman's popularity.
• He was originally conceived as a super *fly* by one of Terry's artists, and changed to a mouse at Terry's suggestion.
• He first appeared in a 1942 cartoon entitled "The Mouse of Tomorrow."
• For his first year of existence, he was called Super Mouse.
• In 1943, Terry changed his name to Mighty Mouse.
• He never spoke in his cartoons until the late '40s, when they became mini-operas.
• He became a TV fixture after CBS bought all of Terry's assets in 1955, to add to their children's programming.

TRIVIA QUIZ

THE SUBJECT IS ...
MICE
Mighty Mouse was one of many popular cartoon mice on TV. How many of these five can you identify?
1. He had his own club on TV (an easy one).
2. He wore a sombrero and was billed as the world's fastest mouse.
3. He was a Japanese mouse who specialized in Judo in the 1960s.
4. He was MGM's brown mouse; he hung around with a Tom Cat.
5. As the cat they tormented would say, "I hate you meeces to pieces!"
ANSWERS:
1. Mickey Mouse
2. Speedy Gonzales
3. Hashimoto Mouse
4. Jerry Mouse
5. Pixie and Dixie

The Mighty Mouse Theme Song

Lyrics and Music: Philip Scheib and Marshall Barer

Mis-ter Trou—ble ne—ver hangs a—round   When he hears this Mi—ght y sound

Here I come to save the day   That means that Mi-ghty Mouse is on his way   Yes-sir

when there is a wrong to right   Mi-ghty Mouse will join the fight

On the sea or on the land, he's got the sit-u—a-tion well in hand

93

The Beany and Cecil Show

THE SHOW: Beany (a freckle-faced boy who always grinned), and Captain Huffenpuff (a benign, slightly inept sailor) travelled the seas in the Leakin' Lena in search of adventure, with Cecil the lovable Seasick Sea Serpent swimming alongside. Cecil and Beany were inseparable buddies who'd do anything to help each other out . . . but it was usually Cecil who came to Beany's aid. In nearly every episode of this weekly cartoon show, Beany was captured by the shifty-eyed bad guy, Dishonest John (NYAH-HA — HA!). And just when it seemed like curtains for Beany-boy, he'd "flip his lid,"

Beany, Cecil, and Captain Huffenpuff

shooting the top of his beany into the air to signal to Cecil that he was in trouble. Then, bellowing "I'm coming, Beany-boy," the sea serpent plowed through the water and arrived just in the nick of time to save his pal . . . whereupon Beany gave Cecil a great big hug, and Cecil gave Beany a big, slurpy kiss. In fact, he gave *everyone* a big slurpy kiss — even D.J., who hated it. "Oh Cees."

THE SONG: Written by the show's creator, animator Bob Clampett.

Main Cast

Beany (a boy)
Cecil the Seasick Sea Serpent
Captain Huffenpuff (Captain of the Leakin' Lena)
Crowy (the lookout)
Dishonest John (the bad guy — NYAH, HA-HA!)

Vital Statistics

Half-hour cartoon show. Syndicated. 78 episodes.
First aired: Jan. 6, 1962
Time slots: Saturday morning, Saturday 7:00 – 7:30 PM (1962)
Last show: Dec. 19, 1964

INSIDE FACTS

**ABOUT ITS CREATOR:
BOB CLAMPETT**

• He was a Warner Brothers animator in the '30s who was instrumental in the creation of all the immortal *Looney Tunes* characters.
• In 1937, he took over the development of Porky Pig and refined him into the humorous stutterer we know today.
• He animated the original Daffy Duck cartoon, *Porky's Duck Hunt*, in 1937.
• He took over Daffy's development in 1938, and teamed him up with Porky.
• He was involved with the creation of Bugs Bunny, and is credited with directing some of the best of all the Bugs Bunny cartoons.
• In 1949, he came up with *Time For Beany*, an Emmy Award-winning TV puppet show that ran until 1955.

TRIVIA QUIZ

**THE SUBJECT IS . . .
WEIRD CARTOON
ANIMALS:**
Cecil's pretty unusual. Here are five other strange cartoon animals. Can YOU name them?

1. A forty-foot purple gorilla.
2. A "sad-sack" shark, who's a pet to four teens with a rock band.
3. An overgrown baby duck who wears a diaper, but is strong enough to lift a car.
4. A horse that wears a mask and bashes bad guys with a guitar.
5. A chicken-hawk who doesn't know what a chicken looks like.

ANSWERS

1. The Grape Ape
2. Jabberjaw
3. Baby Huey
4. El Kabong, better known as "Quick-draw McGraw"
5. Henry the Chicken Hawk, Foghorn Leghorn's nemesis.

Beany and Cecil

Lyrics and Music: Bob Clampett

Come go sail — ing We've wait-ed long e-nough For Bean-y and Cecil, Dis-honest John, and

Cap - tain Huf fen puff. It's time for ad – ven – ture Hot Dog! Some fun! Oh joy!

Crow: Awk!

With Cecil the sea – sick ser-pent And good old Bean — y boy boy boy boy boy

Cecil: Ah - EEE - Ahh - EEE - Ah - CHOOO!

ANNOUNCER: And now, join us for fun with Beany and . . . .

Love-able, gul-li-ble, arm-less, harm-less, ten foot tall and wet Ce-cil the sea-sick sea-serpent — cre-

at-ed by Bob Clam-pett So come on kids, let's flip our lids high-er than the moon Cuz

now here's Bean-y and Ce-cil in (Spoken: A whole half hour) Bob Clam — pett CAR — TOOOOOON Beany: (Laughs)

Lassie

THE SHOW: Timmy and his friend Boomer were exploring a cave they discovered, when Boomer slipped and fell into a giant hole. Now he can't get out! "I think I broke my leg or sump'n," he groans. Luckily Lassie's along. "Quick, Lassie, go get help!" And Lassie zooms off, return a few chilly hours later with the police, an M.D., and June Lockhart in tow. "We were so worried, Timmy. Thank goodness for Lassie!" Super feats like that were standard for America's #1 dog hero. She could catch crooks, foil con men, stop forest fires — you name it. She took care of four different masters, and spent a year alone in the wilds to boot! Here's some shocking news, though — Lassie wasn't a girl. He was a female impersonator. Oh well, no one's perfect.

Lassie and a few of her buddies: Arnold the Pig, Gentle Ben, Judy the Chimp, etc.

THE SONG: An instrumental on the program, but these are the original lyrics. Be sure to have someone shout "Lassie, Lassie!" while you sing it.

Main Cast
Jeff Miller (owner #1): Tommy Rettig
Ellen Miller (his mother): Jan Clayton
"Gramps" (his grandfather): George Cleveland
Timmy (owner #2): Jon Provost
Ruth Martin (his mother; 1957-58): Cloris Leachman
Ruth Martin (1958-64): June Lockhart
Paul Martin (his father; 1957-58): John Shepodd
Paul Martin (1958-64): Hugh Reilly

Vital Statistics
Half-hour adventure. CBS. Syndicated (1971-74)
First aired: Sept. 12, 1954
Time slot: Sunday, 7 – 7:30 PM (1954-71)
Last show: Sept. 12, 1971
Ranked in a year's Top 25: 1958 (22), 1962 (15), 1963 (21), 1964 (13), 1965 (17)

97

INSIDE FACTS

ABOUT LASSIE:
● He was bought for $10 in 1943 by trainer Rudd Weatherwax.
● He first appeared in an MGM movie entitled *Lassie Come Home*, in 1943.
● In the late '40s, MGM gave the TV rights for *Lassie* back to his owner; he developed the series, which was an immediate smash in 1954.
● Lassie chose his first TV "master," Tommy Rettig, from among four finalists for the part.
● At the time, Lassie was 11 years old, and Rettig was 12.
● There were at least six dogs who played Lassie; the original only made the series pilot and never starred in an actual show.
● He was replaced by his offspring, Lassie, Jr.

TRIVIA QUIZ
1. Cloris Leachman, Lassie's second "mom," had her own high-ranking series in the '70s. What was the show?
2. Lassie's third "mom" also had a popular series, a '60s sci-fi program. Can you name it?
3. The 1943 movie, *Lassie Come Home*, featured an unknown child actress who later won two Oscars. Who was she?
4 & 5. Only two TV shows featuring animals as stars have ranked higher in a single year's ratings than *Lassie's* #13 in 1964. Can you name them?

ANSWERS
1. *Phyllis.*
2. *Lost In Space.*
3. Elizabeth Taylor.
4 & 5. *Dáktari* (#7 in 1967), and *Green Acres* (#11 in 1966, #6 in 1967).

The Secret of Silent Hills (The Theme From Lassie)

Lyrics by Charles Newman, Music: William Lava

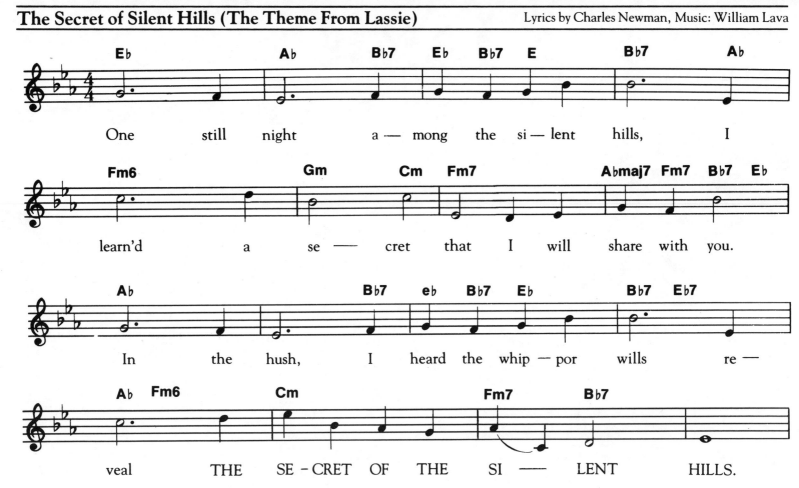

98

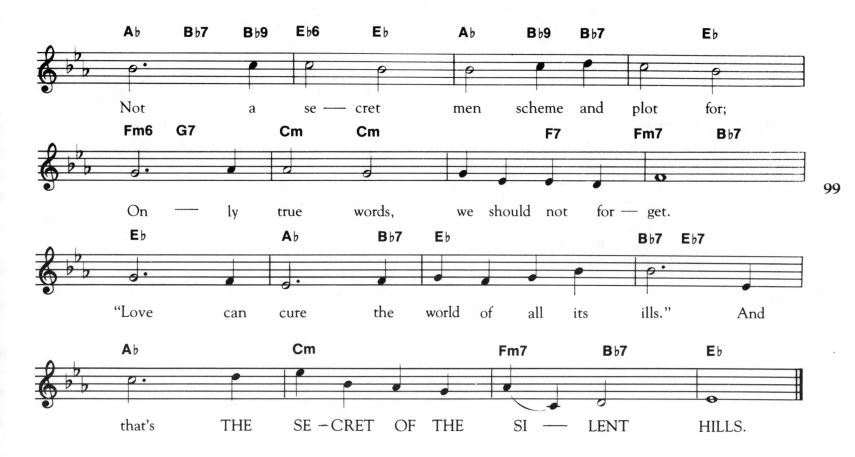

99

Secret Agent

THE SHOW: John Drake, special security agent, is traveling in Europe on a mission for the British government. What mission? Well, who can remember?...Because the most memorable thing about this show was its theme song. *Secret Agent* didn't last too long on American TV — CBS imported it from England for the summer of 1965, and used it again as mid-season replacement in the winter of 1966. But the ratings weren't high enough to warrant its return in 1967. Maybe that was because its star, Patrick McGoohan, insisted that Drake be a "moral man" (he wouldn't carry a

Patrick McGoohan, a. k. a. Secret Agent Man.

gun, and avoided violence and loose women). In any case, it remains one of the few British series to make it into American prime time, and a quality spy show. OF INTEREST: John Drake first appeared in America in 1961 on the short-lived series, *Danger Man*; he last appeared in 1969 as #6 in the TV classic, *The Prisoner*
THE SONG: Co-written by P.F. Sloan, who also wrote *Eve of Destruction*, a #1 song in 1965. *Secret Agent Man* was a #3 song for Johnny Rivers in 1966.

Main Cast

John Drake (secret agent): Patrick McGoohan

Vital Statistics

Hour-long spy/adventure show. CBS. 45 episodes.
First aired: April 3, 1965
Time slots: Saturday, 9 – 10:00 PM (1965), 8:30 – 9:30 PM (1965-66)
Last show: Sept. 10, 1966
Never ranked in the Top 25 shows of a year.

INSIDE FACTS

ABOUT PATRICK McGOOHAN:
● He made his U.S. TV debut eleven years before *Secret Agent*, on a British-produced series called *The Vise*.
● He was a star in England long before he became one in America. By 1960, he had already received an award as Britain's best TV actor, and had been nominated for a similar award as its best stage actor.
● He won an Emmy Award for "Outstanding Single Performance by a Supporting Actor" in 1975, for his role as a criminal in an episode of *Columbo*.
● He created, co-wrote, produced, and starred in one of TV's all-time classics, *The Prisoner*.

TRIVIA QUIZ

**THE SUBJECT IS ...
SPIES**
Secret Agent was one of many spy programs on prime time TV. How many of these shows can you name?
1. A spoof created by Mel Brooks and Buck Henry.
2. It featured an exploding tape recording.
3. A Russian and an American worked together.
4. A tennis pro and his trainer.
5. A millionaire cop became a spy.

ANSWERS
1. *Get Smart!*
2. *Mission: Impossible*
3. *The Man From U.N.C.L.E.*
4. *I Spy*
5. *Amos Burke, Secret Agent* (or *Burke's Law*)

Secret Agent Man

Lyrics and Music: P. F. Sloan and Steve Barri

There's a man who leads a life of danger.
To everyone he meets he stays a stranger.
With every move he makes,
Another chance he takes.
Odds are he won't live to see tomorrow.

Chorus:
Secret Agent Man.
Secret Agent Man.
They've given you a number.
And tak-en 'way your name (Look out!).

Beware of pretty faces you may find.
A pretty face may hide an evil mind.
Ooh, careful what you say;
Don't give yourself away.
Odds are you won't live to see tomorrow.

CHORUS

You're sunnin' on the Riviera one day,
Then bleedin' in a Bombay alley next day.
Oh, don't let the wrong word slip.
While kissin' persuasive lips.
Odds are you won't live to see tomorrow.

CHORUS

Secret Agent Man
Secret Agent Man
This mysterious life you chose
Is a deadly game.

Star Trek

THE SHOW: "Space, the Final Frontier." Representing the United Federation of Planets, the Starship USS Enterprise set out in the 22nd century to explore new life and civilizations. The 400-member crew was led by dashing Captain James T. Kirk, whose poise and courage under pressure was legendary. Second in command: First Officer Spock, a brilliant but emotionless being ("Highly illogical, Captain") with a Vulcan father and an earthling mother. Other trusted crew members: "Bones" McCoy, a stubborn and emotional "country doctor," ("How can you just *stand* there, Spock?!"), Scottie, (the mechanical genius who kept the ship running), Uhura ("All channels are open, Captain"), and the navigators, Sulu and Chekov.

Guess who? It's Leonard Nimoy without Spock's ears!

THE SONG: Co-written by Gene Roddenberry, creator of the series. The lyrics were never used — the melody was sung hauntingly as the Enterprise zoomed through space, leaving the credits in its wake.

Main Cast

Capt. James T. Kirk: William Shatner
Science Officer Spock: Leonard Nimoy
Dr. Leonard McCoy: DeForest Kelley
Lt. Uhura (Communications Officer): Nichelle Nichols
Lt. Commander Scott (Chief Engineer): James Doohan
Mr. Sulu (Navigator): George Takei
Ensign Chekov (Navigator): Walter Koenig

Vital Statistics

Hour-long science fiction show. NBC. 78 episodes.
First aired: Sept. 8, 1966
Most popular time slot: Thursday, 8:30–9:30 PM (1966-1967)
Last show: Apr. 4, 1969
Never ranked in the Top 25 of a year.

INSIDE FACTS

MISCELLANEOUS:

• Believe it or not, the highest *Star Trek* ever ranked in a year's ratings was #52!

• That year it was topped by such memorable shows as *Iron Horse* and *Mr. Terrific* (you *do* remember those, don't you?).

• The original Captain of the Enterprise wasn't Kirk — it was Pike, played by Jeffery Hunter in the first pilot film.

• *Star Trek* was Leonard Nimoy's "first steady job in 17 years."

• William Shatner turned down the lead role in *Dr. Kildare* a few years earlier. Richard Chamberlain got it instead.

• It took three years for Gene Roddenberry to convince a network to air *Star Trek*.

TRIVIA QUIZ

1. What color was Spock's blood?
2. Which crew member was secretly in love with Spock?
3. What was Scottie's first name?
4. In what show did Leonard Nimoy star after *Star Trek*'s demise (hint: he replaced Martin Landau)?
5. What kind of torpedoes did the Enterprise carry?

ANSWERS:

1. Green.
2. Nurse Chapel.
3. Montgomery.
4. Mission Impossible.
5. Proton Torpedoes.

Lyrics: Gene Roddenberry, Music: Alexander Courage

Be-yond the rim of the star-light
My love is wan-dring in star flight.
I know he'll find
In star-clustered reach-es,
Love, strange love
A Star-wo-man teach-es.

I know his jour-ney ends nev-er.
His star trek will go on for-ev-er.
But tell him while
He wanders his star-ry sea,
Remember,
Remember me.

77 Sunset Strip

THE SHOW: Jeff Spencer and Stu Bailey were partners in a high-class Hollywood detective agency located at #77, Sunset Boulevard. Next door: Dino's restaurant, where Gerald Lloyd Kookson III was the parking lot attendant. Stu and Spence tackled every thing from the underworld to glamorous movie stars, but the real key to the show's success was Kookie, whose hip speech and California cool made him a favorite of teenagers all over America. He was in on practically every case, because Warner Bros. was deluged with fan mail whenever he wasn't featured. Also on hand: Roscoe, a horse player, and Suzanne, the luscious French switchboard operator.

The coolest private eye on TV — Kookie!

THE SONG: A jazzy tune with lots of finger-snapping. Written by the authors of many other themes, and these classics: *Cherry Pink and Apple Blossom White, My Own True Love, It Must Be Him, Baby It's You, Close To You.*

Main Cast

Stuart Bailey (detective): Efrem Zimbalist, Jr.
Jeff Spencer (detective): Roger Smith
Kookie (parking lot attendant): Edd Byrnes
Roscoe (a co-worker): Louis Quinn
Suzanne Fabray (the operator): Jacqueline Beer
Rex Randolph (detective): Richard Long
Lt. Gilmore (Hollywood police): Byron Keith
J. R. Hale (parking lot attendant): Robert Logan

Vital Statistics

Hour-long detective show. ABC. 205 episodes.
First aired: Oct. 10, 1958
Most popular time slot: Friday, 9:00 – 10:00 PM (1959-62)
Last show: Sept. 9, 1964
Ranked in a year's Top 25: (1960 (7), 1961 (14)

INSIDE FACTS

ABOUT KOOKIE:

• He was TV's top teen idol for a while, getting 2400 letters a week.
• *Kookie, Kookie, Lend Me Your Comb,* a song he "sang" on the show, became a #4 national hit in 1959.
• The habit of combing his hair was a real one Byrnes used to cover up nervousness.
• Teenage boys copied him, and teenage girl sent him combs in the mail.
• His hip language ("Hey, Daddy-O, meet me at the lid of your cave") sounded natural, but Byrnes actually worked hard at it.
• He said in 1960: "I never talk that way, and the only way I can keep those speeches in my head is to learn them word by word."

TRIVIA QUIZ

"KOOKIE-ISMS" were popular when Kookie was a star of 77. Do you remember what these mean?
1. A Washington.
2. The ginchiest.
3. A dark seven.
4. Pile up the Z's.
5. Mushroom people

ANSWERS:
1. A one dollar bill.
2. The best and grooviest.
3. A bad week.
4. Get some heavy sleep.
5. People who don't come out until night.

77 Sunset Strip

Lyrics and Music: Mack David and Jerry Livingston

Sev·en·ty – Sev·en   Sun-Set   Strip   Sev·en·ty – Sev·en   Sun-Set   Strip

Sev·en·ty – Sev·en   Sun-Set   Strip

The street that wears a   fan cy   la – bel   That's glor·i – fied   in   song and   fa – ble

The most ex ·· cit·ing   peo-ple   pass   you by   In   clu·ding   a   pri — vate eye

Sev·en·ty Sev·en   Sun-Set   Strip   Sev·en·ty   Sev en   Sun-Set   Strip

105

Sev-en-ty – Sev-en   Sun-Set   Strip

You'll meet the   high-brow and the   hip-ster   The star-let   and the   pho-ny   tip-ster

106

You'll see 'most   ev-'ry   kind of   gal   and guy   In --- clu-ding   a   pri — vate eye

Sev-en-ty – Sev-en   Sun-Set   Strip   Sev-en-ty – Sev-en   Sun-Set   Strip

Sev-en-ty — Sev-en   Sun-Set   Strip

Hawaiian Eye

THE SHOW: From their "poolside" office in the posh Hawaiian Village Hotel in Honolulu, Tom Lopaka and Tracy Steele ran Hawaiian Eye, a private detective agency. They hardly ever worked together; each week one of the partners was featured in his own case. But no matter which P.I. was on the job, the main attraction of this show was Hawaii itself. Producer Mark Sandrich explained in 1959: "The scenery is beautiful, the sets are magnificent. And besides, everybody wants to go to Hawaii. We play strictly on that light, vacation level... why, even the 'heavies' are on vacation!" On hand to help: Kim, a wise-cracking, ukelele-playing cabbie in a straw hat, and Cricket Blake, the pretty, young singer at the hotel.

THE SONG: Written by the authors of *77 Sunset Strip*, *Casper the Friendly Ghost*, and many more. Sung by a chorus and accompanied by a Tiki god and Hawaiian scenery.

Hawaiian Eye was Robert Conrad's first TV series.

Main Cast

Tom Lopaka (detective): Robert Conrad
Tracy Steele (detective): Anthony Eisley
Greg MacKenzie (detective): Grant Williams
Cricket Blake (a singer): Connie Stevens
Kazuo Kim (cab driver): Poncie Ponce
Philip Barton (social director): Troy Donahue

Vital Statistics

Hour-long detective show. ABC. 134 episodes.
First aired: Oct. 7, 1959
Most popular time slot: Wed., 9 – 10:00 PM (1959-62)
Last show: Sept. 10, 1963
Never ranked in the Top 25 shows of a year.

107

INSIDE FACTS

MISCELLANEOUS:

• *Hawaiian Eye* was Robert Conrad's first regular TV series.
• He proved to be among TV's most durable stars, with a lead role in four additional prime time series during the next 15 years.
• They included two bombs: *The D.A.* and *The Men*, and two smash hits: *The Wild, Wild West* and *Baa Baa Black Sheep*.
• Connie Stevens was Hawaiian Eye's answer to *77 Sunset Strip*'s Edd Byrnes, providing "teen appeal."
• She had her own hit record in 1960 — *Sixteen Reasons*, which reached #3 on the charts.
• She starred in a short-lived series with George Burns in 1964-65 called *Wendy and Me*.

TRIVIA QUIZ

THE SUBJECT IS...
HIT RECORDS

Connie Stevens capitalized on her TV exposure to come up with a hit record. Can you name these five young stars who did the same?
1. Her show: *The Donna Reed Show*; her hit: *Johnny Angel*
2. Her show: *The Mickey Mouse Club*; her hit: *Tall Paul*
3. His show: *The Rifleman*; his hit: *Cindy's Birthday*
4. His show: *The Donna Reed Show*; his hit: *My Dad*
5. His show: *Then Came Bronson*; his hit: *Long Lonesome Highway*

ANSWERS:

1. Shelly Fabares
2. Annette Funicello
3. Johnny Crawford
4. Paul Peterson
5. Michael Parks

Hawaiian Eye

Lyrics and Music: Mack David and Jerry Livingston

HA –WAI–IAN EYE, _____ HA –WAI–IAN EYE, _____ HA –WAI–IAN EYE,

The

soft is — land breeze brings you strange mel — o — dies And they

tell of ex — ot — ic mys — ter — ies, un — der the trop — i – cal

spell of The HA — WAI–IAN EYE, _____ HA –WAI–IAN EYE,

108

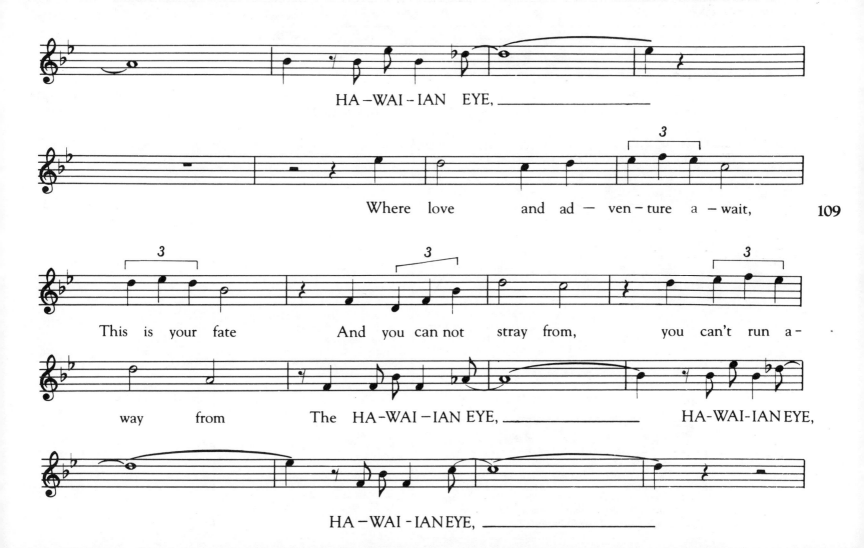

HA –WAI – IAN EYE, _____

Where love and ad — ven – ture a –wait,

This is your fate And you can not stray from, you can't run a-

way from The HA-WAI –IAN EYE, _____ HA-WAI-IAN EYE,

HA –WAI - IAN EYE, _____

Surfside 6

THE SHOW: In 1960, America was starting to go beach crazy. *Gidget* was a hit. Surfing music was popular on the West Coast. The Beach Boys were on the horizon. And on TV, three swinging private eyes who lived on a houseboat in Miami Beach were making waves. Well, not too MANY waves. But *Surfside 6* was popular enough to last for two seasons. Surfside 6 — the guys' telephone exchange — sounded suspiciously like 77 Sunset Strip. There were other similarities: a glamorous location, a chatty, upbeat theme song, and a team of detectives who could trade off as "star of the week". Always on hand: the lovely Daphne Dewitt Dutton, "the girl on the yacht next door", and Cha-Cha O'Brien, a night club singer with a Spanish accent.

THE SONG: Composed by the team who wrote *77 Sunset Strip* and many others. Sung by a chorus as the camera panned across the city, finally focusing on a houseboat moored to a dock.

Troy Donahue thrills a fan in 1960.

Main Cast

Ken Madison (detective): Van Williams
Dave Thorne (detective): Lee Patterson
Sandy Winfield II (detective): Troy Donohue
Daphne Dutton (socialite): Diane McBain
Cha-Cha O'Brien (a friend): Margarita Sierra
Lt. Snedigar (Miami police): Donald Barry
Lt. Plehan (Miami police): Richard Crane

Vital Statistics

Hour-long detective show. ABC. 74 episodes.
First aired: Oct. 3, 1960
Time slots: 8:30 – 9:30 PM (1960-61), 9:00-10:00 PM (1961-62)
Last show: Sept. 24, 1962
Never ranked in the Top 25 shows of a year.

INSIDE FACTS

ABOUT THE STARS:
● When *Surfside 6* debuted, Troy Donahue was a budding teen idol.
● He was a favorite topic of teen fan magazines. Teenaged girls flocked to see him whenever he made personal appearances.
● He was featured on two Warner Brothers detective shows besides *Surfside 6*: *77 Sunset Strip*, as a "long-haired bookworm" (when Edd Byrnes walked out), and *Hawaiian Eye*, as Philip Barton, social director of the Hawaiian Village Hotel (after *Surfside 6* was cancelled).
● Van Williams had played Ken Madison in the same time slot the previous season (1959-60). Only the show was different: *Bourbon Street Beat*.
● He went on to play the Green Hornet in 1966.

TRIVIA QUIZ

THE SUBJECT IS . . . BOATS
The guys' houseboat played a big part in the action of *Surfside 6*. These boats "starred" in TV series, too. Name the series:

1. The Minnow
2. PT Boat 73
3. The Tiki, with Adam Troy, skipper (created by James Michener)
4. A cruise ship that doubles as a floating singles bar
5. The Seaview, a submarine.

ANSWERS

1. *Gilligan's Island*
2. *McHale's Navy*
3. *Adventures in Paradise*
4. *The Love Boat*
5. *Voyage to the Bottom of the Sea*

Surfside 6

Lyrics and Music: Mack David and Jerry Livingston

111

AND NOW...

A Song From A Sponsor

The Armour Hot Dog Song

113

Extra, Extra!
Kid bites dog! Hot Dogs, Ar-mour Hot Dogs — What kind of kids love Ar-mour

Hot Dogs? — Big kids, lit-tle kids, kids who climb on rocks

Fat kids, skin-ny kids, ev-en kids with chick-en pox love hot dogs, Ar—mour

Hot Dogs The dogs kids love to bite!

Alfred Hitchcock

THE SHOW: An anthology of suspense stories with the bizarre twists that were director Alfred Hitchcock's trademark. Each week, "The Master of the Macabre" would appear with a droll "Good Evening", and introduce the night's melodrama. He also made an appearance before each commercial break, warning viewers that they were about to watch the most horrific part of the program — a word from the sponsor (which, he told *TV Guide*, the sponsors did not find funny for the first few years). Actually, Hitchcock had little to do with the production of the series. As "executive producer", he directed only twenty of the episodes in ten years and left the rest to his hand-picked crew. He did retain final say over story selection, however, believing that this was the key to a successful show.

THE SONG: Adapted from a classical piece, "The Funeral March of the Marionette", by Gounod.

Goood EEEvening.

Main Cast

The host: Alfred Hitchcock (Good Eev'ning)

Guest stars: Steve McQueen, Joanne Woodward, Dick York, Peter Lorre, Dick Van Dyke, Robert Redford, Claude Rains, Barbara Bel Geddes, and hundreds more.

Vital Statistics

Half-hour/hour suspense show. CBS/NBC. 361 episodes.
First aired: Oct. 2, 1955
Most popular time slot: Sunday, 9:30 – 10:00 PM (1955-60)
Last show: Sept. 6, 1965
Ranked in a year's Top 25: 1957 (6), 1958 (12), 1959 (24), 1960 (25)

INSIDE FACTS

MISCELLANEOUS:

• Hitchcock's face was well known to film fans. But after he began appearing on television regularly, crowds started recognizing him.

• He related in 1959 that while filming on location, he overheard a passerby say: "Look Maude, there's Hitchcock of TV! Now what do you suppose he's doing on this movie set?"

• Most of the story ideas for his program came from short stories and novels. He believed that if someone had a really good idea, they wouldn't use it in a TV script — they'd save it and use it in their own work.

• One year, his staff read over 400 hundred novels before they found 32 stories they could use.

TRIVIA QUIZ

Hitchcock is famous for his movies. Here are scenes out of five of his most famous films. Can you identify them?

1. Cary Grant in a chase on Mount Rushmore
2. A memory expert spouting classified information in a theater.
3. An attack on Rod Taylor by a flock of animals
4. Lawrence Olivier and Joan Fontaine watching a mansion burn
5. An injured James Stewart intently watching Raymond Burr.

ANSWERS

1. *North By Northwest*
2. *The 39 Steps*
3. *The Birds*
4. *Rebecca*
5. *Rear Window*

The Theme From Alfred Hitchcock

Transcribed by Stanley Wilson

115

117

Dragnet

THE SHOW: A stark, realistic police drama — the first to show cops as regular working men who had to put up with the "day-to-day drudgery" of their jobs. Jack Webb played the no-frills Sgt. Joe Friday ("Just the facts, ma'am") with a straight face and a monotone. He also produced, directed, and co-wrote the series, basing each episode on an actual case from the files of the Los Angeles Police Department. (". . . The story you are about to see is true; the names have been changed to protect the innocent.") Each week Friday and his partner — there were five of them in eleven

Dragnet: The ultimate cop . . . Sgt. Joe Friday. DUM DE DUM DUM.

years — methodically sorted through clues, leads, and potential witnesses until they finally got their man! DUM DE DUM DUM!

THE SONG: It was a million-seller by The Ray Anthony Orchestra, reaching #3 on the charts in 1953. It's one of TV's best known instrumentals, particularly the end. Sing along, now: DUM DE DUM DUM.

Main Cast

Sgt. Joe Friday: Jack Webb
Sgt. Ben Romero (Partner #1): Barton Yarborough
Sgt. Ed Jacobs (Partner #2): Barney Phillips
Officer Frank Smith (Partner #3): Herb Ellis
Officer Frank Smith (Partner #4): Ben Alexander
Officer Bill Gannon (Partner #5): Harry Morgan

Vital Statistics

Half-hour police drama. NBC.
First aired: Jan. 3, 1952. **Returned:** Jan. 12, 1967
Time slots: Thurs., 9 – 9:30 & 8:30 – 9:00 PM (1952-58),
9:30 – 10:00 PM (1967-70)
Last show: Sept. 6, 1959   **Last show:** Sept. 10, 1970
Ranked in a year's Top 25: 1953 (4), 1954 (2), 1955 (3), 1956 (8),
1957 (11), 1969 (20)

INSIDE FACTS

**THE ORIGIN
OF THE SHOW:**

• It happened on the set of a 1948 movie called *He Walks By Night*, a realistic police drama in which Jack Webb played a police officer.
• Webb was chatting with the film's "technical adviser," an L.A. police sergeant. He wondered aloud whether a radio show based on real-life police cases would work. The sergeant believed it would.
• Encouraged, Webb produced a sample show and NBC bought it, complete with Webb starring as Friday. Webb then approached the L.A.P.D. Chief, who agreed to supply case histories.
• It was a hit on radio, so Webb's sponsors asked him in 1951 to develop it into a TV show as well.
• DUM DE DUM DUM.

TRIVIA QUIZ

1. What was Friday's badge number?
2. At the end of each program, the name of Webb's production company was chiseled into a block of stone. What was the name?
3. Finish this *Dragnet* phrase: "This is the city — Los Angeles, California. I work here, I _____ ."
4. Webb created another cop show, starring Martin Milner as Peter Molloy, which ran from 1968-75. What was it called?
4. *Dragnet* was among the Top 10 shows of a year four times. Only one other cop show has matched that record. Which one?

ANSWERS

1. 714.
2. Mark VII.
3. ". . . carry a badge."
4. Adam 12.
5. Hawaii 5-0.

The Dragnet March ("Danger Ahead")

Music: Walter Schumann

119

AND NOW...

A Song From A Sponsor

The Gillette Look Sharp March

Written by Mahlon Merrick

To look sharp ev — ry time you shave,

to feel sharp, And be on the ball,

just be sharp, use Gil — lette Blue

Blades for the quick — est slick — est shaves of all

121

Perry Mason

THE SHOW: It's Saturday night, and 25 million people are watching as Perry Mason takes on another case. It looks bad for Perry's client, of course. Lt. Tragg has gathered enough evidence to make any *normal* defense attorney beg for mercy. D. A. Hamilton Burger, who has lost every case for the last five years, is gloating: "Your client hasn't got a chance, Perry," he smirks. In the courtroom, witnesses place Mason's client at the scene of the crime, and at least one has overheard his client threatening the murder victim. Perry stays calm. During the recess for lunch, Perry huddles with Paul Drake. "Paul, find out who owned the blue sedan parked in front of the victim's house on the night of the murder." "Right, Perry." During the cross-examination, Drake returns. "Here it is," he says, handing Mason a piece of paper. The audience knows what's coming: a courtroom confession. "I didn't want to kill him, but he was *laughing* at me . . ." Case closed.

Perry Mason, about to spring the trap . . .

THE SONG: No words to this one, but get someone to play it and hum along — you know how it goes!

Main Cast

Perry Mason: Raymond Burr
Della Street (Girl Friday): Barbara Hale
Paul Drake (detective): William Hopper
Lt. Tragg (L.A. police): Ray Collins
Hamilton Burger (D.A.): William Talman

Vital Statistics

Hour-long lawyer/detective show. CBS. 271 episodes
First aired: Sept. 21, 1957
Most popular time slot: Saturday, 7:30 – 8:30 PM (1957-62)
Last show: Sept. 4, 1966
Ranked in a year's Top 25: 1959 (19), 1960 (10), 1961 (16), 1962 (5), 1963 (23)

INSIDE FACTS

HOW BURR BECAME MASON:
• An established film actor, he was tired of playing the "heavy" (a typical Burr role: the killer in Hitchcock's *Rear Window*).
• He wanted to be Perry Mason so he could be a hero for a change.
• Seriously overweight, he isolated himself in a cheap hotel for six months until he was thin enough to look the part of Mason.
• The show's producers thought he would make a great Hamilton Burger, but Burr refused. They compromised: the producers let him try out for Mason and he agreed to test for Burger.
• It was up to Erle Stanley Gardener, Mason's creator, to pick the star.
• As soon as he saw Burr's screen test, he jumped up, yelling, "That's him!" The rest is TV history.

TRIVIA QUIZ

1. William Hopper, who played P.I. Paul Drake, was the son of what famous Hollywood personality?
2. Which *Perry Mason* regular was a star in the movie *Godzilla*?
3. Who played the judge in the last episode of *Perry Mason, The Case of the Final Fadeout*?
4. In 1973, CBS tried to revive *Perry Mason* with a new star. Who was he?
5. Mike Connors and Walter Pidgeon hold what distinction in *Perry Mason*'s history?

ANSWERS
5. They were the only people to replace Burr in a *Perry Mason* episode.
4. Monte Markham. It bombed.
3. Erle Stanley Gardner, Mason's creator.
2. Raymond Burr.
1. Hedda Hopper.

Perry Mason Theme

Music: Fred Steiner

123

124

125

You Bet Your Life

THE SHOW: Here's how you played *You Bet Your Life*. First, there was the secret word. "It's a common word, something you see every day" (a stuffed duck with a strong resemblance to Groucho was lowered from the ceiling with the word pinned to it). If one of the contestants said the word, they won an extra $100. Next, a pair of contestants came on stage, ready to answer four questions in a category they had selected, to try to win some money. But even though the questions were fairly simple, it wasn't *easy* money . . . because they had to survive a grilling by Groucho Marx before they got a chance to play the game! That was what the show was *really* about. And it was so much fun to watch Groucho torment his guests that *You Bet Your Life* became the highest-rated prime time quiz show in TV history.

THE SONG: Performed as an instrumental on the show, it was originally featured as a vocal (sung by Groucho and cast) in the Marx Brothers' 1930 film, *Animal Crackers*.

The inimitable Groucho

Main Cast

MC: Groucho Marx
Announcer: George Fenneman

Vital Statistics

Half-hour quiz show. NBC.
First aired: Oct. 5, 1950
Most popular time slot: Thursday, 8:00-8:30 PM
Last show: Sept. 21, 1961
Ranked in a year's Top 20: 1951 (16), 1952 (9), 1953 (9), 1954 (4), 1955 (4), 1956 (7), 1957 (18), 1958 (10)

INSIDE FACTS

ABOUT THE SHOW:

● *You Bet Your Life* is shown frequently as reruns. This is possible because it was always filmed instead of being broadcast live.

●This enabled the show's producers to delete Groucho's off-color comments, and to edit out all but the funniest parts.

● A classic true story: Groucho always asked his contestants what they did for a living. In the late '50s one man answered that he was a writer who had been working on a novel. His name was William Peter Blatty. The novel he was working on was *The Exorcist*.

● In 1980, *You Bet Your Life* was resurrected, with Buddy Hackett as the host. Without Groucho, the show didn't make it.

TRIVIA QUIZ

**THE SUBJECT IS . . .
GAME SHOWS**

Guess the show:
1. Three guests claim to be the same person.
2. One member of a two-person team tries to get his partner to say a specific word, giving one-word clues.
3. Panelists Cerf, Kilgallen, etc. try to figure out a guest's special trait or ability.
4. Three panelists try to guess the cost of an item. The closest guess without going too high wins.
5. The audience humiliates itself for a chance to peak behind door #3.

ANSWERS:
1. *To Tell The Truth.*
2. *Password.*
3. *I've Got a Secret.*
4. *The Price Is Right.*
5. *Let's Make A Deal.*